International Library of Philosophy and Theology

MODERN THINKERS SERIES

David H. Freeman, Editor

TOYNBEE

TOYNBEE

by

C. GREGG SINGER

PRESBYTERIAN AND REFORMED PUBLISHING CO.
Nutley, New Jersey
1977

CONTENTS

The Author _____ 6

A Selected Bibliography _____ 7

Introduction _____ 9

The Background of his Philosophy _____ 11

Toynbee's Method _____ 13

The Rise of Civilizations: Basic Assumptions _____ 14

The Breakdown of Civilizations _____ 17

The Disintegration of Civilization _____ 31

The External Proletariat _____ 40

Schism in the Soul _____45

Toynbee and his Critics _____ 67

Conclusion _____ 74

THE AUTHOR

Dr. C. Gregg Singer is a graduate of Haverford College and received his Ph.D from the University of Pennsylvania. Since 1958 he has been chairman of the history department at Catawba College, Salisbury, North Carolina. Prior to this he served in a similar capacity at Wheaton College, Salem College, and Bellhaven College. He is the author of *A Theological Interpretation of American History* in the *Philosophical and Historical Studies Series* in the International Library of Philosophy and Theology.

A SELECTED BIBLIOGRAPHY

America and World Revolution, New York, Oxford University Press, 1962.

Christianity and Civilization, Wallingford, Pennsylvania, 1947.

Christianity Among the Religions of the World, New York, Scribner's, 1957.

Civilization on Trial, New York, Oxford University Press, 1948.

An Historian's Approach to Religion, New York, Oxford University Press, 1956.

The Pattern of the Past; Can We Determine It? Boston, Beacon Press, 1949.

A Study of History, 12 volumes, New York, Oxford University Press, 1934-1961. (The same abridged by David Somervell in two volumes.)

The World and the West, New York, Oxford University Press, 1949.

Gargan, E. T., *The Intent of Toynbee's History*, Loyola University Press, 1961.

Montagu, M. F., *Toynbee and History: Critical Essays and Reviews*, Porter Sargent, Boston, 1956.

Note: *A Study of History* in 12 volumes and the very excellent abridgment by David Somervell and approved by Toynbee are the keys to his interpretation of history. His other works, for the most part, are simply specific applications of material which are contained in his massive *Study of History*.

INTRODUCTION

Arnold Toynbee is undoubtedly the most important philosopher of history yet to appear in the twentieth century. His prominence lies not only in the popular appeal which his works have gained, but also in the very nature of the interpretation of history which they represent. Towering above Spengler, Sorokin, and Herbert Butterfield, he has sought to give to contemporary man a panoramic conception of the whole of the human past and, unlike most historians, he has not confined his efforts to the history of one nation, era, or race. Allowing his photographic imagination to rove at will over the human past, he has endeavored to bring it all within the synthetic confines of a sympathetic treatment which would give it meaning and which at the same time would be amenable to the dictates of the techniques of the best of contemporary scholarship. Toynbee not only set out to free the study of history from the prison house of determinism in which it had been confined by the Marxists and Spengler, but also to rescue it from the pitfalls of a meaningless existentialism which makes a mockery of the idea of history. In short, Toynbee addressed himself to a task of such magnitude that would have discouraged many a scholar of lesser dedication to the cause of historical scholarship, for any synthetic approach to history creates problems so formidable that many, if not most, historians hardly dare to engage in such a task and much prefer to act as critics for those who do undertake such a project.

The historian who would dare to enter upon the task of presenting an acceptable philosophy of history in the manner of Toynbee must not only possess a thorough knowledge of

9

the human past, but he must at the same time be equally at home in the field of philosophy. For the task which he has chosen as his own particular domain in the world of scholarship, Arnold Toynbee brought with him peculiar gifts and a background of knowledge in the classics which have made his *A Study of History* the great achievement of the twentieth century in the field of historical interpretation.

Born in London in 1889, Toynbee was educated at Winchester and Oxford, from which university he was graduated in 1911. In this same year he studied at the British Archaeological School in Athens and this experience gave him an enduring interest in the history of classical civilization which later furnished the inspiration for his *A Study of History*. At the same time, however, he became interested in the current British political scene as a result of a conversation he overheard in a cafe. Upon the outbreak of World War I, he served with the Political Intelligence Department of the British Foreign Office. As a result of this experience he was named a delegate to the Versailles Conference of 1919, as a specialist on the Middle East. These wartime experiences, particularly those associated with the writing of the peace treaty, served to bring to his thinking a new awareness of the continuity within history and a realization that the events he was witnessing were not unrelated to the history of Greece and Rome. Returning from Paris, he became professor of Byzantine and modern Greek languages and history at the University of London, in which position he served until 1924. From 1925 until 1955 he served as director of studies for the Royal Institute of International Affairs and as Research Professor of International History.

Arnold Toynbee thus entered upon his role as a philosopher of history with a background of formal training both in the classics and in the practical knowledge of the world since 1914, which is rather unique among historians. But this unusual combination of an intimate knowledge of the classical past and contemporary problems has given him that panoramic conception of history which is absolutely necessary for a sound interpretation of historical data. And yet this very strength in Toynbee's basic training also seems to be one of his weaknesses as well, for it seems to have tempted him to use the history of Greece and Rome as a frame of reference

10

or model for the interpretation of all the other civilizations he discusses on the dubious assumption that hellenistic culture furnishes the true pattern which all other civilizations must follow.

Although Toynbee has proven to be a prolific writer, this analysis of his philosophy will be largely based on his monumental *A Study of History,* the first three volumes of which appeared in 1934 and the final volume, *Reconsiderations,* in 1961. His other works, for the most part, are simply more detailed studies of the various aspects of the broader treatments contained in his major work. These other works will be used as occasional references to shed further light on his major effort.

THE BACKGROUND OF HIS PHILOSOPHY

Although the roots of his interest in the meaning of history are undoubtedly to be found in Toynbee's early devotion to the study of classical culture and his intimate connections with the Paris Peace Conference of 1919, there were other important influences at work on his thinking, and he has admitted these with great candor ("I Owe My Thanks," *Saturday Review,* October 2, 1954, pp. 13-16, 52-55). In this article he thanks Edward Gibbon for showing him what an historian can do, and Sir Edward Creasy for his *The Fifteen Battles of the World* which he feels gave him his first notion of the possibility of a universal history. He has also admitted his debt to C. G. Jung for his psychological insights and he even pours out his gratitude to Plato for teaching him to use his imagination as well as his intellect, and to Robert Browning for his concept of challenge and response. For various other reasons, he admits the influence of John Stuart Mill, Theodore Mommsen, Goethe, and Heine. He is also grateful to Herodotus and the Gospels for giving him an awareness of what he delights to call the divine being in history. And in a final gesture of generosity, he thanks World War II for allowing him to see that the world of 1914 was entering upon experiences which Thucydides had already recorded.

In spite of this generosity in his recognition of these philosophers and historians of whose influence he is conscious as

11

molders of his own thinking, it is highly doubtful that this list of acknowledgements is either accurate or complete. It is quite obvious that Toynbee has missed the real meaning of the Gospels on the one hand and that he has failed to recognize the influence which Henri Bergson has exercised upon him on the other. And it is highly doubtful that Toynbee is as free from the influence of Spengler as he would like his readers to believe. There is something more than a mere suggestion of Bergson's conception of the *l'elan vital* in his concept of challenge and response in the growth of a civilization and the imprint of Spengler's *Decline of the West* is visible in Toynbee's *A Study of History*, in spite of the author's conscious effort to escape the rigid determinism which marked the approach of Spengler toward the problem of the rise and fall of civilizations.

The philosophical and historical backgrounds of Toynbee's work are so varied and the influences at work in its production are so complex that it is difficult to categorize Toynbee's position as a philosopher of history, although it is the personal position of the author that Toynbee is more greatly influenced by "process" philosophy than by any other school of thought. Yet it is also true that mysticism and empiricism, determinism and libertarianism, Christianity and paganism, and classicism and modernism are all in competition with each other throughout the twelve volumes of this important study as clues to the mystery of the drama of the human past. These competing systems not only give Toynbee's approach an amazing variety of insights, but also an equally puzzling inconsistency as one philosophy gains the ascendency in his thinking. It is also to his credit that Toynbee makes no attempt to conceal the fact that his philosophy has changed at certain vital points since he first began to write his monumental study and he freely admits this fact in his *Reconsiderations*. But the greatest change in his position is his attitude toward Christianity, in that he has virtually repudiated it as his own personal religion. Such a drastic reversal of his original position in turn has vitally affected some of his basic conclusions in regard to the role of the church in the rise of a new civilization out of the ruins of the old.

Toynbee's approach to the interpretation of history is through the examination of the rise and fall of civilizations. A civilization is the smallest unit of historical study at which one arrives when he endeavors to come to an understanding of the history of his country. But these intelligible units are neither nations nor states (nor mankind as a whole), but a certain grouping of humanity into societies or civilizations and, viewed in this light, they serve as the basis for his approach to a discovery of the meaning of history. Toynbee has been criticized at this point for the reason that his definition of a civilization is artificial and that his efforts to apply it consistently to all of the societies he brings within the orbit of his study lead to some serious distortions, particularly when he ventures into the unfamiliar areas of Far Eastern history.

Using it as his guide, however, Toynbee finds that there have been thus far in history twenty-one civilizations, of which five (or seven) are still alive. In addition to these twenty-one fully developed civilizations, Toynbee found five others which he calls abortive or arrested.[1] These arrested civilizations do not play an important role in Toynbee's thinking, for he insists that the fully developed cultures have emerged from the primitive societies, and the emergence of a civilization from such a primitive state is an arduous achievement which constitutes one of the major themes in his interpretation of the historical process.

Toynbee insists that these twenty-one civilizations are to be studied empirically in terms of the laws of growth and decay and it is for this reason that his history of civilizations has been described as a chronicle play in two acts, which in turn consist of an almost infinite number of scenes. Act One features the growth of civilizations and is built around the basic theme of challenge and response. Act Two describes and features their disintegration. Act One comes to an end when a challenge arises to which the civilization in question fails to offer an adequate response. This is the critical moment in the history of the civilization and disintegration

---

[1] He also admits that there have been about 650 primitive societies which for various reasons never developed into civilizations.

sets in at that point in its history. Act Two is longer than Act One for the decline which now ensues is by no means an uninterrupted movement downward, for it is marked by rallies and succeeding relapses. Toynbee devotes a much greater portion of his *Study of History* to the lengthy processes of decline than he does to the emergence of these civilizations.

THE RISE OF CIVILAZATIONS: BASIC ASSUMPTIONS

Underlying this empirical approach to the problem of the rise and decay of civilizations is the assumption that their emergence out of the state of a primitive society is to be attributed to a process which Toynbee calls challenge and response. Toynbee insists that the growth of a civilization—this process by which it emerges out of the state of a primitive society— is initiated by a creative minority which is able to lead the society to making a successful response to an initial challenge and then to a series of such challenges which can be natural, physical, or human in their nature. These successful responses are the result of the ability of the creative minority to call forth the willing cooperation of the uncreative majority.

Toynbee is convinced that civilizations are born in environments which are unusually difficult and not unusually easy in their nature—by which he means that either material or human factors must be present which are of such a nature as to call forth significantly successful responses to the challenges they present to society. The most stimulating challenge, however, is a kind of golden mean. An excessive challenge may be so severe that the society in question cannot meet it with the necessary successful response. A challenge that is too severe may even break the spirit of the challenged society so that it becomes arrested in its development. On the other hand a deficient challenge may fail to call forth a response of sufficient force to promote the growth of the challenged society into a civilization.

Toynbee probes still further into the nature of his theory of challenge and response and sets forth still another requirement for the ideal challenge. If it must not be either too

14

severe or too easy, neither can it be of such a nature that it merely calls forth one successful response. Rather must it be able to call forth in the challenged society a momentum of sufficient strength to carry it a step further: from one achievement to a fresh struggle; from the solution of one problem to the confrontation of another. In all of this there must be sufficient momentum to convert the movement generated by one successful response into a repetitive and recurrent rhythm.

At this point in the presentation of his theory of the rise of civilizations, Tonybee relies heavily on Bergson's concept of *élan vital* to account for the repetition of successful responses to a series of meaningful challenges. Toynbee believes that this *élan vital* works through what he calls a series of overbalances. Each overbalance exposes the emerging civilization to fresh challenges and thereby inspires fresh responses. One overbalance sets up the necessary conditions for the next overbalance, and this process, according to Toynbee, is potentially infinite in spite of the fact that growth and decay are the underlying assumptions of his empirical approach to the interpretation of history. As proof of the effectiveness of the *élan vital* working through a series of overbalances, Toynbee appeals to the course of Hellenistic civilization, in which he professes to see its influence from its genesis up to its zenith in the fifth century B.C.

The effective response on the part of a society to a series of challenges, according to Toynbee, is not the result of a determinism at work in the historical process, even though this might seem to be his position at this point because of his reliance on Bergson. Rather are these effective responses the result of the effective work of a creative minority within the society which formulates the response. The essential factor in this development of a civilization lies in the fact that a passive majority willingly accepts the leadership of this creative minority in meeting the challenges coming to the society.

Toynbee devotes Volume Three of his *A Study of History* to an analysis of the growth of civilizations and he assigns a dominant role in it to these creative minorities. He takes particular care to define what he means by a creative minority. It is, at least, and at best, a very small part of the total members of any given society and its influence is in no way

✳ essential factor = passive majority
willingly accepts leadership

dependent on its numerical strength. The influence of this minority depends on the almost mystical relationship which its members are able to achieve over the passive majority. It is for this reason that, in spite of the fact that this creative minority is hopelessly outnumbered by the uncreative masses, it is able to exercise an effective leadership and bring about successful responses to the various challenges which confront a society.

But how is this creative minority able to exercise this leadership? How does it secure the cooperation of the inert masses in the venture of creating a civilization out of a primitive society? The answer to these questions is basic to the understanding of Toynbee's thesis concerning the growth of civilizations. For the answer he leans heavily on Bergson, who insisted that the mystics are the superhuman creatures par excellence. From this Toynbee has come to the conclusion that a dynamic society arises somehow in the emergence of mystically-inspired personalities who by the very nature of their inspiration are creative. These creative personalities are impelled to transfigure their fellow men into fellow creatures by recreating them in their own image. On the basis of these Bergsonian presuppositions Toynbee finds the answer to his basic problem. It is the privilege and the task of the creative minority to transfigure the inert majority by recreating it in its own image. This process is the very essence of the rise of civilizations out of primitive societies. If the creative genius fails to bring about such a transformation, his own creativeness will be fatal to him. In the same manner, the creative minority must bring about a transformation of the majority in an emerging society or all is lost.

But how does this transformation of the inert majority take place? Toynbee admits that all works of social creation are either the product of individual creators or of creative minorities, and at each successive advance of a society the vast majority of its members are left hopelessly behind in its cultural achievements And in this fact lies a great danger to any civilization. Toynbee goes so far as to say that this is the real danger which faces the West today—that the majority is to a great degree isolated from any real participation in the advance of culture, not in the sense of creating it,

16

but in the sense of comprehending and appreciating the work of the creative minority.

Of course, this is a danger which has faced every civilization that has successfully emerged from the state of a primitive society in history as it is thus far recorded. Toynbee has found a solution to the problem of bringing the uncreative rank and file of any society into a meaningful contact with a creative minority of pioneers by what he calls mimesis, a kind of social drill which leads the majority to the acquisition of certain social assets, aptitudes, emotions, or ideas. In mimesis, the inert majority imitates the creative minority. But Toynbee also admits that mimesis is a kind of short cut to the development of a civilization in any society and, as such, it may be a dubious expedient since it almost always exposes a growing civilization to the peril of breakdown.

But as long as the creative minority is able to cope with the challenges that arise to confront it, the civilization of which it is a part will continue to develop. But this creative minority must be able to secure the willing allegiance of the uncreative majority if it is to be able to continue offering successful responses. When in the history of any civilization, the creative minority is no longer able to secure this willing allegiance from its followers, it is in serious danger of a breakdown and Toynbee devotes the rest of his original ten volumes to this problem.

THE BREAKDOWN OF CIVILIZATIONS

Toynbee insists that the problem of the breakdown of civilization is more obvious than their development. Of the twenty-six civilizations which he includes in his study, he declares that sixteen are dead and buried. The ten survivors are our own society (Western society), the main body of orthodox Christendom in the Near East, its offshoot in Russia, the Islamic society, the Hindu society, the main body of the Far Eastern society in China, its offshoot in Japan and the three arrested civilizations of the Polynesians, the Eskimos, and the Nomads. Toynbee then pushes his investigation a step further and goes on to say that if we will take a closer look at these ten, we will see that the Polynesian and Nomad

17

societies are now in their last agonies and that seven of the remaining eight civilizations are all to varying degrees facing the stroke of either being annihilated or assimilated by our own Western society. Toynbee affirms further that six of these seven show signs of having already broken down and having entered into a state of disintegration. The one exception is the Eskimos, whose civilization was arrested in its infancy.

On what basis does Toynbee come to conclusions that lead to the suspicion that he is quite pessimistic about civilizations in general? Indeed, it is difficult to escape the conclusion that the breakdown of civilizations have a kind of fatal fascination for this philosopher. In his survey of contemporary cultures he discovers many more evidences of decay than he does of growth. Toynbee holds that one of the most conspicuous marks of breakdown in a civilization is a phenomenon which takes place in the last stage of its decline and fall—its forcible unification into a universal state. The obvious disintegration of the society tempts the society to purchase a kind of reprieve from its fate by resorting to a universal state imposed by force. He finds the classic example of this use of the universal state in the Roman Empire into which the Hellenic society was forcibly gathered up in the "penultimate chapter of its story." But this plunge into a universal state has not been a remedy sought by the Hellenic society alone. Orthodox Christendom entered into such a state in the shape of the Ottoman Empire at the end of the fifteenth century after the political unification of Muscovy and Novgorod. The Hindu civilization found its universal state in the Mughal Empire and its successor, the British Raji. The main body of the Far Eastern civilization likewise found a similar remedy for its problem in the Mongol Empire and its resurrection under the Manchus while the Japanese offshoot entered into the Tokugawa Shogunate, and thus toward its ultimate decline.

At this point, Toynbee is encouraged to venture the opinion that there is an ideological premonition of the universal state for the Islamic society in the Pan Islam movement, and he then proceeds to use this accumulation of instances of a universal state as evidence for the conclusion that all the six extant non-Western civilizations have broken down internally before they were broken in upon by the impact of Western civilization from the outside. From this conclusion he points out a further generalization that any civilization which becomes the victim of a successful intrusion from without has already broken down internally. This kind of reasoning logically forces Toynbee to one further observation, namely, that all of the living civilizations, except for our own Western, have already broken down internally and are in the process of disintegration.

But what about our Western civilization? Where does it stand? Has it also entered upon the process of a disintegration in some way only faintly discernible at the present time? Toynbee admits that it manifestly has not yet entered upon the era of a universal state, but his point is that such an era is not the only evidence of a process of disintegration already under way. The entrance upon a universal state is preceded by what Toynbee calls a "time of troubles" and he then offers a cautiously worded possibility that if we were to judge the present state of Western civilization by the purely subjective criterion of our own feelings about our own age, "we would undoubtedly conclude that the time of troubles has descended upon the West."

Why do civilizations enter into these long and painful periods of disintegration? Are they a necessary and inescapable aspect of the stuff and essence of the historical process? What forces are at work in human affairs which bring them about? Toynbee is not unaware of the force of these questions at this juncture in his study, and he deals with them openly, if not always convincingly. He feels that the major factor in the breakdown of any civilization is the loss of creative power in those creative individuals that are the minority. But why do they lose their creative power? Must this loss necessarily take place in all civilizations? The very fact that Toynbee admits that the process of breakdown is visible in all extant civilizations except our own, and that it has been a decisive factor in those civilizations of the past which have already broken down, raises some very serious questions. Likewise, his admission that the West seems to be entering upon a time of troubles brings Toynbee perilously close to a kind of determinism as the explanation of the rise and fall of civilizations. And he is not unaware of the impasse to which his observations and candid admission point.

19

In Volume Four of his *A Study of History* he attempts to deal with the intriguing questions which have haunted all the philosophers who have sought to explain the rise and fall of civilization in terms of certain elements common to all men, without yielding, at the same time, to the demands of a philosophical determinism.

Toynbee laments the fact that it is one of the perennial infirmities of human beings to ascribe their own failures to forces beyond their control, and he admits that this kind of mental maneuvering is particularly attractive to sensitive minds in periods of decline and fall. Toynbee insists that such an attitude was common during the decline of classical civilization, but at the same time he insists that modern physical science has rendered any similar view or feeling untenable today as far as the immediate, and even the far distant, future are concerned (Somervell, I, p. 247).

Having disposed of those determinists who associate the breakdown of civilizations and relate the destinies of human institutions with the destinies of the universe as a whole, Toynbee then turns his attention to another breed of determinists who appeal to the law of senescence and death with a shorter wave length "for which they claim jurisdiction over the whole kingdom of life on this planet." In this connection he singles out Spengler for being guilty of a foolish dogmatism because he sets up a metaphor and then proceeds to argue it from a law based on observed phenomena. In opposition to Spengler, Toynbee categorically denies that societies are living organisms and can thus be subjected to biological laws. To declare that every society has a predestined time span is as foolish as it would be to declare that every play has to have just so many acts (Somervell, I, p. 248).

In the same manner Toynbee rejects that type of determinism that asserts that there is an inevitable process of deterioration in which the qualities of the individuals which participate in the civilization breakdown, and thus the breakdown of the civilization occurs.

Equally unacceptable to Toynbee is the cyclical view of history, although he admits that in the movement of Yin and Yang, challenge and response, withdrawal and return—the forces that weave the web of history—there is the obvious element of the recurrence of events. But he denies that this

20

process of recurrence can be termed cyclical since in all of this process there is a developing design and not simply an endless repetition of the same pattern. The detection of periodic repetitive movements in the process of civilizations does not in any way imply that the process in itself is of the same cyclical order as they are. The major movements in the stream of historical events are progressive. "Humanity is not an Ixion bound forever to his wheel, nor Sisyphus forever rolling his stone to the summit of the same mountain and helplessly watching it roll down again" (Somervell, I, p. 254).

Toynbee closes this part of his study on the optimistic note that Western civilization is not confronted with any "Saeva Necessitas." It is not doomed by necessity to join the majority of its species. "Though sixteen civilizations may have perished already to our knowledge, and nine others may now be at the point of death, we—the twenty-sixth— are not compelled to submit to the riddle of fate to the blind arbitrament of statistics" (Somervell, I, p. 254). Toynbee is convinced that the divine spark of creative power is still alive in Western society and that if we have the grace to kindle it into a flame, the stars in their courses cannot defeat our efforts to attain the goal of human endeavor. These passages in which Toynbee rejects these four versions of determinism are among his most eloquent and will undoubtedly win both the hearts and the minds of those who rightly share his fears of any determinism which is born of a natural law philosophy.

But in spite of this heart-warming eloquence, it is doubtful that Toynbee has solved the problem as thoroughly as he seems to feel. These passionate outbursts against determinism do not of themselves free him of his own version of this approach to history. For the thoughtful reader, there must still be a lurking suspicion that Toynbee is caught in the mesh of another form of determinism and may not be entirely aware of his own shortcomings at this point. It should be noted that he does not offer any solution to the problem of determinism. He merely denies it as an interpretation of the historical process. As a matter of fact, he merely denies certain forms of this dogma, but not all of the basic possible variants of this theme.

Actually, Toynbee quite frequently throughout *A Study of History* breathes the spirit of Bergson's version of the theory of emergent evolution and he apparently feels that this reliance upon the doctrine of the *élan vital* frees him of any suspicion of yielding to the influence of determinism.

But is emergent evolution as used by Bergson any less deterministic than the other forms of naturalism and evolutionary thought? This question can only be answered in the negative. In spite of the language in which it is cloaked, it must be assumed that Bergson's version of the evolutionary philosophy is ultimately no less deterministic than those forms which are more obviously so. To the degree which any philosophical system depends upon the evolutionary hypothesis, to this same degree it opens itself to the charge of determinism.

The inherent determinism and resulting pessimism springing from a reliance upon the position of Bergson is evident in Toynbee's candid admission that the sixteen civilizations have already perished and that nine others seem to be at the point of death. His one consolation is the hope for Western man that he has the grace to kindle that divine spark of creative power which is still alive in him. This is, to say the least, a fragile hope, and its fragility becomes obvious in the light of the discrepancies which are to be found in Toynbee's earnest endeavor to escape the results of a deterministic philosophy without denying its roots.

Having disposed of the deterministic theories of the breakdown of cultures (at least to his own satisfaction), Toynbee then turns to an actual examination of the process which brings them to their ruin. In a very true sense, his rejection of determinism as a solution to the problem actually enhances the difficulties confronting him in his explanation of the phenomenon of the breakdown of civilizations. It opens up to him a whole vista of possibilities, and the remainder of the *A Study of History,* in one way or another, is given over to their examination. Toynbee's rejection of the theory that the breakdown of civilizations can be traced back to the operations of cosmic forces which are beyond human manipulation and his insistence that it is caused by those factors over which man may have some controlling interest and influence renders his task much more complex. To insist that factors essentially human are responsible for the breakdown of civilizations is to open the door to a multiplicity of possible causes for this phenomenon in human history.

Toynbee then turns to an examination of the possibility that civilizations die because they lose control over their physical and human environments. In considering whether the loss of control over the physical environment can be considered as a cause of decline, Toynbee insists that the degree of command which any society possesses over its physical environment can be measured by its techniques and then quickly arrives at the conclusion that there is little, if any, relationship between the development of techniques and the actual health of any given society. As evidence for his position, he cites cases in which techniques have actually been improving while civilizations either remain static or are in a state of decline. In this connection he also admits there have been situations in which the techniques of society have remained static while the society in question has either gone forward or declined. The examination of many instances where he feels there is no relationship between techniques and the health of a society leads Toynbee to the conclusion that when a breakdown in a civilization is contemporary with a decline in a technique, the latter is a consequence or symptom of the former, rather than its cause.

Toynbee then turns his attention to the consideration of the rather widely held theory, popularized by Gibbon in his *Decline and Fall of the Roman Empire,* that civilizations decline because of their loss of control over their human environments and that they fall because of the fact that they cannot withstand assaults launched upon them by alien enemies. To refute this theory, Toynbee found it necessary not only to rehearse the facts connected with the downfall of his various societies, but also to date the beginning of their downfall in a somewhat arbitrary manner suitable for his purposes. In fact, his system of dating is not only somewhat arbitrary, but also rather unscientific. He finds, for instance, the beginning of the breakdown of Orthodox Christian Society in 977, in the Russian branch of Christendom in 1675, in the Far Eastern in 878, in the Far Eastern in Japan in 1185, in the Hindu civilization in 1175, and he places the breakdown of Islamic society in 1500. This early dating for the downfalls of these various societies may surprise many Toynbee readers, but

23

then it must be remembered that he finds the beginning of their breakdown in the early stages of their respective developments. His arbitrary handling of this problem is quite obvious in his insistence that Hellenic culture entered upon its period of breakdown some four hundred years before Rome was founded. His early dating for the beginning of the fall of classical culture leads Toynbee into an unusually harsh attack on Gibbon's *Decline and Fall of the Roman Empire,* with the caustic comment that it never occured to Gibbon that the age of the Antonines was not the summer, but actually the Indian summer, of Hellenic history and the degree of Gibbon's hallucination is betrayed by the very title of his work.

In the light of his examination of the barbarian invasions of Rome and other invasions which accompanied the decline of other civilizations, Toynbee returns a negative verdict as to their complicity in the actual breakdown. He concludes that the loss of command over the human environment has no more to do with the breakdown of a civilization than does its loss of control over its physical environment. "In all the cases reviewed, the most that an alien enemy has achieved has been to give to the expiring suicide his *coup de grace"* (Somervell, I, p. 272).

Although he concedes that thus far history and his inquiry into the reasons for the decline and breakdown of civilizations have yielded only negative results, Toynbee is also convinced that his analysis of alien assaults upon a civilization has also produced valuable clues looking toward the solution of the problem. These clues in turn lead to a further examination which centers around mimesis, which he defines as that relationship which exists between the creative minority and the uncreative majority, and which lies at the heart of the emergence of all civilizations. At this point Toynbee creates a paradox in his system. This process of mimesis, upon which he places such great importance, has a radical weakness. Just because it is a kind of drill for the training of the uncreative majority, it is at the same time a mechanization of human life and there is present in its use a great risk of catastrophe. Toynbee's excuse for its use in spite of the perpetual and imminent threat which it presents is simply that a growing society is compelled to live dangerously.

Creative minorities or personalities in the vanguard of a civilization who have used the mechanism of mimesis expose themselves to two certain risks, one negative in character and the other positive. Toynbee finds that the risk of negative failure lies in the fact that the creative leaders may infect themselves with the very hypnotism which they have induced in their followers and in this case the docility of the masses is purchased at the disastrous price of the loss of leadership by the creative leaders. Toynbee is convinced that this is the explanation for arrested and stagnant behavior.

But this loss of leadership by hypnosis is not the end of the story. When the leaders cease to lead in the sense that they can no longer secure the willing response of the uncreative majority, their tenure of power becomes an abuse for the majority, which turns into a revolt, and the leaders seek to restore order by drastic action. At this point Toynbee finds the use for which he has been searching, and calls this reaction the positive failure. By this he means that the military formation previously in force breaks down into anarchy. It is the disintegration of a brokendown civilization which makes itself evident in the secession of the proletariat from a band of leaders who have degenerated into a dominant minority. The dominant minority now seeks to achieve by force what the creative minority was formerly able to achieve by a willing acceptance of its leadership on the part of the masses.

When such a secession takes place, the result is a loss of harmony in the society in which it occurs. This loss of harmony further results in a corresponding loss of self-determination on the part of that society. Toynbee holds that this loss of self-determination is the ultimate criterion of growth. Toynbee is nothing less than logical in admitting that the loss of this prized possession is the sign of breakdown.

How does this loss of self-determination through the disappearance of harmony within society become evident? It becomes apparent when the attempt is made to introduce into a society new social forces which the existing set of institutions was not designed to handle. Toynbee calls this effort to introduce new institutions pouring new wine into old bottles. This effort may take the form of an adjustment, a revolution, or an enormity. These are the three possible answers for a society challenged by the introduction of new

25

social forces. If a harmonious adjustment takes place, the society will continue to grow; if the revolution comes, its growth will become extremely hazardous; if enormities occur, the breakdown of that society in which they occur is imminent.

Toynbee looks on revolutions as retarded and proportionately violent acts of mimesis in that every revolution has reference to something that has already happened. They are violent because they are, according to Toynbee, belated triumphs of powerful new social forces over tenacious older institutions which have been able to thwart, at least temporarily, these expressions of a new form of social life.

Social enormities are the penalty which a society is called upon to pay when the act of mimesis which was designed to bring about harmony of the older social institution with a new social force is not simply retarded but is frustrated entirely.

Toynbee then cites industrialism and democracy as two new dynamic social forces which have been set in motion over the last two centuries and proceeds to examine the question as to how the West has endeavored to meet the challenge which they have offered. His method is to offer a comparison of the effects which both of these forces have exerted on both slavery and war. The answer which the West found for the challenge to slavery was its abolition but, as yet, the West has not been able to find a satisfactory answer to the challenge of war. Toynbee, with a note of pessimism at this point, admits that whether the West will succeed in achieving a type of successful response to this challenge which has never been achieved by any other civilization is a question that "lies on the knees of the gods." There is no doubt that he is keenly aware of the fact that the West has failed at this point and he plunges into a discussion as to why this is the case.

He finds his answer to this important question in the fact that before democracy collided with the institution of war, it already had come into conflict with the institution of parochial local sovereignty. The attempt to import the new driving forces of democratic industrialism into the old machinery of the parochial state has generated the twin enormities of political and economic nationalism. The unfortunate result of this process is modern total war because the parochial states have become nationalistic democracies.

This thesis is too neatly arranged to satisfy most of his readers. There is in it, of course, something more than a germ of truth. There is no doubt that modern technology has greatly increased the war potential of even the smaller states. But Toynbee draws too sharp a distinction between the old parochial state and the new industrial democracy with its strongly nationalistic overtones. Nationalism can hardly be said to be a product of the era since the Industrial Revolution, and not all the parochial states have become democracies, however nationalistic they may be. This over-simplification of the history of the past three centuries fails to come to terms with the forces at work in modern society which have really produced the problem of total war. If political and social nationalism are truly the enormities which Toynbee considers them, he has failed to offer a satisfactory explanation for their appearance.

In a somewhat similar manner Toynbee points out that contemporary society is confronted with the task of adjusting the old institution of private property as an institution likely to be found in societies in which the single family household is the normal unit of economic activity to new conditions. In such a society Toynbee concedes that it is possibly the most satisfactory system developed for the distribution of material wealth under such an agrarian type of society (Somervell, I, p. 290). But Toynbee also insists that our modern Western economy has transcended the family unit, and the family institutions of private property and society must come to terms with this fundamental change in the economic structure. The method of peaceful readjustment is to counteract the maladjustment of private property which industrialism inevitably brings in its wake. It achieves this goal by arranging for a deliberate, rational, and equitable control and redistribution of private property through the agency of the state. Toynbee sees an additional advantage in this method of meeting the challenge of industrialism in that it transforms the state from being an agency largely devoted to the purpose of war into an agency whose main function will be the advancement of the common welfare.

He offers the prediction that if this peaceful adjustment should fail, then the revolutionary alternative will overtake the West in some form of communism, for the maldistribution of property resulting from the impact of industrialism on a society essentially agrarian would otherwise be an intolerable enormity if its effects should not be effectively mitigated by an extension of social service by the state and a program of higher taxation.

Toynbee candidly admits that the revolutionary remedy found in communism might well prove to be a little less deadly that the disease which it is intended to cure, since the institution of private property is so closely related to all that which is best in our pre-industrial heritage. Thus its abolition would probably produce a disastrous break in the social tradition of Western society. In the light of this admission it becomes doubtful that Toynbee can really offer any meaningful solution to the dilemma that he foresees for the West. He is tacitly admitting that there is actually not too much difference between his program for the redistribution of private property through the agency of the state and the communist program for the forceful seizure of such property for redistribution which is more far-reaching. But this communist approach could be even more fatal than the enormity which now confronts the West.

It is apparent that at this point Toynbee is confronted with a tremendous difficulty and to a large degree it is of his own making. It can be noted that the essentially pragmatic character of his philosophy comes to the forefront of his thinking in the assumption that the institution of private property is basically a social convenience, a product of a certain society, but which, nevertheless, has contributed much to our heritage. Thus to surrender the practice of private property is to endanger a set of values derived from a previous age to which it contributed so much. Toynbee's basic failure at this point lies in his inability to recognize that private property is not merely an institution created by man for his own convenience at a particular period in his development, but rather that it is a divinely ordained means for maintaining social order in a sinful humanity. Thus Toynbee does not oppose communism on moral or religious grounds, but simply from the point of view of social convenience, namely, that its program for the seizure of private property could endanger certain attitudes and values deeply ingrained in our Western society.

In his rather long section in which he deals with the failures of self-determination as a possible cause for the breakdown of civilizations, Toynbee offers the conclusion that it seems as if it were uncommon for the creative minority to offer more than two successful responses to two or more successive challenges in the history of civilization. Indeed, the party that has distinguished itself in dealing with one challenge frequently fails in meeting the next one. He is even willing to claim that this is one of the principal themes of the New Testament. He feels that this particular phenomenon which he calls the mimesis of creativity is a very potent cause for the breakdown of civilizations. He also insists that this failure brings on breakdowns in two very distinct ways.

In the first place, it reduces the number of possibilities for playing the role of creator since it frequently rules out those who have successfully responded to the succeeding challenge. In the second place, those who have thus been disqualified now appear in the front rank of the opposition to those who replace them as the leaders in meeting the next challenge. Toynbee ascribes their opposition to the new leadership to the fact that they have become victims of an infatuation with the past which he calls the sin of idolatry— the worship of the creature rather than of the creator. Although we may object to Toynbee's use of an analogy to describe their plight, there is obviously a real truth to be found somewhere.

This mimesis of creativity may take two forms, either the idolization of an ephemeral self or the idolization of an ephemeral institution. And even though this mimesis of activity may seem to be a highly artificial interpretation, Toynbee would take issue with such a judgment as being premature and would summon an interesting array of witnesses in defense of his position.

He insists that the Children of Israel are the most notorious example of the idolization of the ephemeral self, and he finds evidence of this charge against them in the New Testament. This is, to say the least, a novel view of the New Testament indictment of the Hebrews as a people. Toynbee also declares that Athens, Virginia, and South Carolina are guilty of this kind of idolization. On the other hand, he exonerates North Carolina from any complicity in the guilt of her neighbors.

Toynbee holds that Hellenic society was guilty of the idolization of an ephemeral institution and in being guilty it paid a very high price for the crime—its own breakdown. He finds similar instances in the total infatuation of Orthodox Christendom with the ghost of the Roman Empire. This is a classic example for him of the idolization of an institution.

Societies can also come to grief because they idolize an ephermeral technique and this likewise results in a mimesis of creativity. At this point, Toynbee summons the theory of biological evolution as evidence to support his thesis and then specifically names the Nomads and the Eskimos as cases in point. He charges that because of their excessive concentration of all their faculties on the techniques used in the care of sheep and in hunting they condemn themselves to retrogression toward animalism, even as the fish of the sea, achieving a similar success in adapting themselves to their marine life through the acquisition of fins, condemned themselves to be left far behind in the evolutionary struggle when they achieved a complete success in adapting themselves to their marine life in this achievement. But Toynbee is able to find another and more modern instance of the idolization of techniques in the case of those British industrialists who idolized obsolescent techniques in the twentieth century simply because these same techniques had brought fortunes to their grandfathers in the preceding era.

Toynbee now turns from these passive methods of yielding to the mimesis of creativity to what he calls the active aberrations which he defines in terms of three Greek words, *koros*, *hubris* and *atē*. To each of these he assigns both subjective and objective meanings. Objectively, *koros* means sinful, *hubris* outrageous, and *atē* disaster. Subjectively, *koros* means the psychological condition of being spoiled by success, *hubris* the consequent loss of moral and mental balance, while *atē* means the blind, headstrong, ungovernable impulse which sweeps the unbalanced soul into attempting the impossible. Toynbee indicates that he derived the theme involved in these three terms from Athenian tragic drama of the fifth century. Using examples from the military history of Assyria, Charlemagne, and France and England during the Middle Ages, he comes to the conclusion that military action throws much light on the fatal chain of *koris, hubris,* and *atē,* because military skill and prowess are edged tools which are quite likely to inflict fatal injuries on those who misuse them.

But a more fatal form in which the tragic chain presents itself is in the intoxication which accompanies victory, whether the struggle in which the fatal prize is won is a war of arms by men or a conflict of spiritual forces. Toynbee insists that both variants of this drama can be found in the history of Rome; the intoxication of a military victory from the breakdown of the republic in the second century B.C. and the intoxication resulting from a spiritual victory from the breakdown of the Papacy in the thirteenth century. Toynbee arrives at this latter concept of spiritual victory by a somewhat arduous and unrealistic line of thought. He insists that the victory that Gregory VII won for the Hildebrandine ideal ultimately brought about the triumph of the world, the flesh, and the devil over the City of God during the fourteenth century when the Papacy "became possessed by the demon of physical violence it attempted to exercise" (Somervell, I, p. 353).

THE DISINTEGRATION OF CIVILIZATION

In Volume Five of his *A Study of History* Toynbee passes from an investigation of the breakdown of civilizations to the problem of their ultimate disintegration and he feels that this stage of their development and history poses questions similar to those which arise when developing civilizations pass from their genesis into an era of growth. And even as the problem of the growth of a civilization must be kept separate from that of its genesis, so must the problem of its breakdown be studied as a process distinct from their disintegration. Even as some civilizations had somehow managed to solve the problems of genesis, but failed to solve the problem of growth and thus became arrested civilizations, so other civilizations after a period of time and breakdown suffered a similar arrest and enter upon a long period of petrification.

31

This injection of the problem of arrested development and disintegration into the study of civilizations is not an accidental analogy which Toynbee creates for some kind of balance in his study of the rise and fall of cultures. This is far from being the case. Actually, it is one of the most important aspects of his whole approach in the development of a philosophy of history. In his insistence that certain civilization are arrested in their development while others are arrested in their disintegration, Toynbee is actually attacking the problem of determinism and its role in the processes of history once again from a somewhat different angle. Even as growth does not inevitably follow the genesis of a civilization, neither must disintegration, necessarily follow a breakdown. The rise and fall of civilizations cannot be a mechanical process and Toynbee returns to this theme again in Volume Six to give it even fuller treatment. Nevertheless, this similarity of stages in the rise and fall of civilizations is for Toynbee a kind of parallelism which he finds useful. In each case there is a series of challenges, but in its period of growth a civilization successfully meets them through an *élan vital* which carries the challenged party into an overbalance which declares itself in the manifestation of a new challenge. In the case of disintegration, the repetition of challenges still takes place, but now the responses fail, and here is the major difference between the process by which a civilization arises and by which it declines.

During disintegration the repetition of challenges still takes place, but now the responses are unsuccessful. But the process is somewhat different from the process which take place during the rise of a civilization. In place of a series of challenges, each different in character from its predecessor which has been successfully met and relegated to past history, during disintegration the same challenge is presented again and again. Toynbee insists that when the outcome of each successive encounter is defeat rather than victory, the unanswered challenge can never be disposed of and it is bound to present itself again and again until it either receives some tardy and imperfect answer or else brings about the destruction of the society which has shown itself incapable of making a successful response.

At this point the question may very well be asked: Why
is this challenge bound to present itself again and again until
it receives some imperfect answer or destroys the society in
question? Why must this be the case? Is there some deterministic principle at work which makes this process inevitable? It is obvious from the previous discussion that
Toynbee would not accept such an answer to the question. He
offers his own answer which is quite obviously based on his
empirical study of the twenty-one civilizations which have
already perished. He comes to the conclusion that it does
take place in every disintegrating civilization without exception. But he is not unaware of the pitfall which lies ahead
in this kind of reasoning and he assigns causes to this process
of disintegration which, to his satisfaction, maintain a degree
of human freedom throughout history. Whether or not Toynbee is successful in his defense of human freedom against
historical determinism in its various forms is an important
question which will be discussed later in more detail. But
Toynbee is never unmindful of the necessity of such a defense
when he seems to verge on the precipice of determinism in
seeking answers to such questions.

In his study of the disintegrations of civilizations, Toynbee follows the same essential pattern which he uses in
tracing their growth. The result is an interesting parallel.
He begins his analysis of the process of disintegration by
looking for a criterion by which he may judge it before he
examines the process as a whole in such a manner as he looked
for a similar criterion of growth before embarking upon that
portion of the study. And just as he came to the conclusion
that the criterion of growth was not to be found in an increasing command which a society achieves over its physical
or human environment, so he comes to a similar conclusion
that the loss of such a command cannot be regarded alone as
the cause of disintegration. He even feels that the available
evidence suggests that an increasing command over these environments is a concomitant of disintegration rather than of
growth. In support of his position he cites the resort to
militarism and insists that although this policy is frequently
a feature of the breakdown and disintegration of societies,
it is, nevertheless, frequently effective in increasing the command which they exercise over the forces of nature and other

33

living societies. A society which has become incurably divided against itself is almost certain to devote for militaristic purposes the major part of their additional natural and human resources which the increasing command has made available. As evidence for this tendency toward self-destruction Toynbee points to the resources which Alexander the Great achieved and which were wasted in futile civil wars by his successors and also the misuse of the resources accumulated by Rome during the second century B.C. in the civil wars which followed and which ultimately brought forth the empire under Caesar Augustus.

Having dismissed these possible explanations for the disintegration of societies as insufficient, Toynbee proceeds to find his criterion elsewhere and the next clue he follows is the spectacle of that division and discord within the bosom of a society "to which an increase in its command over its environment can so often be traced back" (Somervell, I, p. 356). He uses this for the ultimate criterion and fundamental cause of the breakdown which precede the disintegration of a civilization. The outbreak of internal discord brings with it the loss of the faculty of self-determination in the society which suffers the domestic turmoil.

These social schisms or discords are of two varieties, vertical schisms which occur between geographically separated communities and those which are horizontal in nature. This latter type takes place in communities which are geographically intermingled but composed of socially segregated classes.

The vertical type of schism manifests itself most frequently in a reckless indulgence in the crime of interstate warfare. Toynbee feels that this is a kind of main line of suicidal activity for civilizations. But, at the same time, he insists that this vertical schism is not the most characteristic manifestation of the schism and discord by which the breakdown of civilizations are brought about. He argues that the articulation of a society into a parochial community is common to the whole genus of human societies, civilized and uncivilized. Warfare between states is merely an abuse of a potential instrument of self-destruction which is within the reach of any society at any time.

34

Toynbee emphasizes a phenomenon which he delights to call a horizontal schism. This type of division along the lines of class is not only peculiar to civilizations, but it is also a phenomenon which appears at the moment of their breakdown and thus becomes a distinctive mark of this period of breakdown and disintegration. Horizontal schisms are characterized by the appearance of two groups, an internal proletariat and an external proletariat. Looking once again to the classical era for support for his position, he describes the architects or creators of the Christian Church as the internal proletariat of Hellenistic society, and the creators of the barbarian war bands which invaded the Roman Empire constitute the external proletariat. Both of these proletariats arose during a "time of troubles" in which the Hellenistic society was no longer creative and already in a state of decline and both of these secessions of the two kinds of proletariats were provoked by a previous change in the character of the ruling body. And once again Toynbee appeals to Hellenic history for his evidence. The creative minority which had at one time been able to secure a voluntary allegiance from the uncreative masses within the Hellenic society because of the very charm which was its prized possession gave way to what Toynbee calls the dominant minority, and this change brought about a new era in the history of that society. This dominant minority, destitute of the charm which characterized it in a former period of leadership and now uncreative, sought to retain its privileged position by force. The secessions of the war bands and the Christian Church were reactions to the tyranny now exercised by the dominant minority within that society. The dominant minority in attempting by perverse methods to hold this disintegrating Hellenic society together actually defeated its own intentions. But in so doing it left a monument to itself in the creation of the Roman Empire, which actually appeared before either the Christian Church or the war bands (external proletariat). The dominant minority thus encased itself in a universal state in the form of the Roman Empire.

In his study of the disintegration of civilizations, Toynbee places much emphasis on the results of the appearance of a horizontal schism. In fact, the appearance of this phenomenon is the essential key to his whole theory of the declines of civilizations, and the importance which he attaches to this factor is clearly evident as he traces the influence of three groups which emerge at this point in the history of a civilization—the dominant minority and the external and internal proletariats. Toynbee calls the existence of these three groups a social schism, and he further breaks this down into two additional factors: schism in the body social and schism in the soul. He insists that this social schism must not be treated lightly for it is the product of two negative movements within the society, each of which he feels is inspired by an evil passion.

First, the dominant minority attempts to hold by sheer force the privileged position which it has ceased to merit and which is no longer willingly accorded to it by the passive masses. This resort to the use of force in turn causes the proletariat to repay injustice with resentment, fear with hatred, and violence with violence. Yet, in spite of this, the whole movement ends with positive acts of creation—the universal state, the universal church and the previously mentioned war bands. Toynbee states his case at this point as follows. History clearly reveals to us in the phenomenon of disintegration a movement that runs through war to peace; through Yin to Yang; and through and apparently wanton and savage destruction of precious things to fresh works of creation that seem to owe their special quality to the devouring glow of the flame in which they have been forged (Somervell, I, p. 369).

At this point Toynbee would appear to be on the verge of a pessimism born of a kind of determinism in the process of Yin and Yang, but his essential optimism and evolutionary outlook come to his rescue. If disintegration were wholly destructive, it would not only be very difficult, but also quite impossible, for a new civilization to emerge out of the debris of the old one. If such an emergence were not possible Toynbee's basic concept of the evolution of human culture would become quite untenable and there would be little basis upon which any distinction between his position and that of Spengler could be drawn.

There is in Toynbee's position a very close relationship between schism and rebirth (palingenesis) and this rebirth takes place even during the period of disintegration since the dominant minority creates not only a universal state, but

36

also a higher philosophy while at the same time, the internal proletariat brings forth a universal religion. Toynbee is rather generous in his admiration for these dominant minorities and their ability to produce an admirable governing class. He claims that out of twenty civilizations that have broken down, no less than fifteen have produced universal states as they have traversed the road that leads almost inevitably to their ultimate dissolution. He is able to find the universal state of Hellenism in the Roman Empire, a Babylonic in the reign of Nebuchadnezzar, an Egyptian in the Middle Empire of the eleventh and twelfth dynasties, a Russian Orthodox in the Muscovite Empire, and he is even able to discover a universal state for the main body of Orthodox Christendom in the Ottoman Empire. In the Far East he finds that the Mongol Empire in China and the Tokugawa Shogunate in Japan are the examples.

The creative power of these dominant minorities is not confined to the political arena alone for in at least four cases Toynbee declares that they have also produced a distinctive philosophy, the most important illustration of which is the Greek philosophy produced by the Hellenic dominant minority.

When Toynbee turns from the dominant minorities to the proletariats of the disintegrating society he finds that there are diversities, although within the range of this spiritual diversity, the external and the internal proletariats are at opposite ends of the pole, but the degree of diversity is greater among the external proletariats.

Although once again he summons ancient history as his witness for this thesis concerning the role of the internal proletariats, he lays greater emphasis than usual on the history of the West where there is an overwhelming abundance of evidence. He claims that our Western civilization has drawn upon the manpower of no less than ten disintegrating civilizations to conscript them into the Western body social during the past four hundred years. But Western society has not been content to prey upon its own kind and has rounded up for use nearly all of the remaining primitive societies. For the North American Indian this conscription has been a blow almost too great to survive, but somehow the Negroes of Africa have survived this process of recruitment in a manner apparently not possible for the unfortunate Indians.

At this point in his argument, Toynbee presents one of the most challenging aspects of his whole concept of disintegration. In brief, he argues that the dominant minority recruits an intelligentsia from the internal proletariat as an agency for continuing its control. The first such recruits are military and naval officers who are followed in turn by the diplomats and then the merchants. The function of these three groups is to learn as much of the domineering society's arts of war, diplomacy, and commerce as is necessary to save their respective peoples from conquest. It was for such a purpose that Peter the Great learned the art of Western warfare so as to save Russia from Sweden.

But the process of recruiting ideas does not stop at this point. As the leaven of the virus of Westernism works deeper into the life of the society which is being permeated and assimilated, the intelligentsia develops its most characteristic types, the schoolmaster who has mastered the practice of teaching Western subjects, the civil servant who has mastered the practice of conducting the public administration according to Western forms, and finally the knack of applying a version of the *Code Napoleon* in accordance with French judicial procedure. Where there is such intelligentsia present, not only have two civilizations been in contact, but also one of the two is in the process of being absorbed into the internal proletariat of the other.

Because of its role in society, this intelligentsia, acting as a kind of liaison class, is never happy. It suffers from the congenital unhappiness of the hybrid that is an outcast from both of the families that have conspired to beget them. An intelligentsia, argues Toynbee, is hated and despised by its own people because its very existence is a reproach to them. It is a living reminder of the hateful, but inescapble, alien civilization which cannot be ignored and must be humored.

He finds a contemporary illustration of this dilemma in the very heart of the Western civilization as well in the semi-Westernized fringes in the lower middle class which has received a secondary and even a university education without being given any corresponding outlet for its trained abilities. This middle class, Toynbee insists, was the backbone of the Fascist Party in Italy as well as of the Nazi Party in Germany.

In his survey of Western history Toynbee finds many sources for the recruitment of this internal proletariat and comes to the conclusion that while the evidence of the recruitment of an internal proletariat is at least as abundant in the recent history of the Western world as it is in that of any other civilization, there is singularly little evidence pointing to the emergence of a universal church or any proletarian-born higher religions (Somervell I, pp. 400-401).

This admission forces Toynbee to the further admission that the series of parallels which he claims to have found between our own and Hellenic society breaks down because of this one fundamental difference. The Hellenic society did not take over any universal church. Today, the situation is quite different, for parochial paganism certainly was not characteristic of our own civilizaton which Toynbee admits was once entitled to call itself Western Christendom. He is also convinced that the West, in spite of the efforts of Descartes, Hobbes, Voltaire, Marx, Mussolini, and Hitler to de-Christianize it, still carries the virus or elixir of Christianity in its blood and that it is very doubtful that the spiritual condition of the West can ever be refined to a paganism of Hellenic purity.

As far as the United States is concerned, Toynbee offers the interesting observation that the conversion of the Negro slaves to the Christianity of their masters is that kind of miracle which brings healing to the familiar schism which exists between the proletariat and dominant minority and that this healing has taken place in spite of the fact that the dominant minority in the West has been endeavoring to repudiate Christianity. In view of this revival of Christianity among the Negroes, Toynbee optimistically declares that the sap of life is visibly flowing once again through all the branches of Western Christendom. This revival suggests that the next chapter in the history of the West may not follow the lines of the final chapter of Hellenic society. "Instead of seeing some new church spring from the ploughed soil of an internal proletariat in order to serve as the executor and residuary trustee of a civilization that has broken down and gone into disintegration we may yet live to see a civilization that has tried and failed to stand alone being saved in spite of itself from a fatal fall by being caught up in the arms of

39

an ancestral church which it has vainly striven to push away and keep at arm's length" (Somervell, I, pp. 402-403).

With another burst of optimism, Toynbee points out that if this is actually the case, then this tottering Western civilization may be reprieved of a death sentence which it imposed upon itself, that is, of treading out the tragic path of disintegration and he sees the possibility that an apostate Western Christendom may be given grace to be born again as Republica Christiana "which was its own and earlier and better ideal of what it should strive to be" (Somervell I, p. 403). In this connection Toynbee raises the same question, quite out of context, which Nicodemus asked the Lord, and he applies Christ's answer that a man must be born again to enter into the Kingdom of God to the problem of the survival of man, and of the West. Toynbee means that only by a spiritual rebirth can the West hope to survive, but he does not have a spiritual or Biblical meaning in mind when he uses Christ's answer to Nicodemus as the solution to the dilemma of the West.

THE EXTERNAL PROLETARIAT

The external proletariat, like its internal counterpart, comes into existence by an act of secession from the dominant minority of a civilization which has already broken down. There is, however, one very important difference between these two groups. Whereas the internal proletariat continues to be geographically intermingled with the dominant minority from which it is separated by a moral gulf, the external proletariat is both physically and morally separated from the dominant minority by a frontier which can be traced on a map. Indeed, for Toynbee, the crystallization of such a frontier is a sure indication that such a secession has already taken place. As long as a civilization is still growing, it has no well-defined geographical boundaries, except at those particular points at which it comes into conflict with another civilization of its own species.

This lack of well-defined boundaries in a growing civilization results from the fact that a creative minority which is successfully performing its role has a power of radiation so great that it permeates the primitive societies which surround it. In fact, Toynbee argues that it would be impossible to find a primitive society which has not been permeated to some degree by a creative minority of a growing civilization. This radiation of a growing civilization consists of three elements; the economic, the political, and the cultural, and these seem to be radiated with equal power and exercise equal charm. But as soon as a civilization ceases to grow, the charm of its culture begins to evaporate. However, its powers of economic and political radiation may and probably will continue to grow faster than ever. But since the cultural element is the true essence of a civilization and the economic and political elements are only relatively trivial manifestations of its cultural depths, it follows that even the most spectacular triumphs of its economic and political systems are at best imperfect and precarious.

What happens at this point is as follows. The external proletariat no longer imitates the arts of peace, the basic culture of the broken-down civilization, but it does continue to imitate the improvements, the technical gadgets in the arts of war, industry, and politics. It does this not for the purpose of becoming one with the broken-down civilization which it is imitating, but that its members may more effectively guard themselves against the violence which is by this time the most conspicuous characteristic of the broken-down civilization. Between the dominant minority and the external proletariat there now exists a kind of military frontier and across this line a baffled dominant minority and an unconquered external proletariat now face each other. This military frontier constitutes a barrier to the passage of all social radiation, except that of military techniques. Toynbee contends that this type of military and social exchange makes for war, rather than peace.

For historical evidence of his position, Toynbee once again cites Hellenic civilization. However, he also finds an interesting parallel in the history of the West and its contact with primitive societies in its early stage in the charm which Western Christendon exercised on pagan groups. But this peaceful penetration of primitive groups by Christianity finally gave way to force. The first chapter of the expanse of Western Christendom into Britain was the peaceful conversion of the English by a band of missionaries from Rome,

41

but later, coercion was used, beginning with the decision of the Council of Whitby of 664. Toynbee also uses British imperialistic expansion in India as further evidence for the pattern which is first discernible in the Hellenic past. His conclusion is that in this world-wide Western offensive against the rear guard of primitive societies, extermination, eviction or subjugation have been the rule, and conversion the exception. Toynbee can think of only three such examples—the most important of which is the case of the Scot Highlanders.

But what does this almost complete overthrow of these external proletariats mean to a civilization? In view of the success of the West in eliminating the various barbarian groups with whom it has come into contact, should we rejoice in the conclusion that the West is safe? Toynbee can give only a negative answer to this question. The destruction which has overtaken many of the civilizations of the past has come from within rather than from without. He insists that we will have gained nothing "if the barbarians in their hour of extinction beyond the frontiers have stolen a march on us by re-emerging in our midst." It is his conviction that this is the very real threat which we now face in the West.

Having reached this point in his thinking, Toynbee makes a dramatic concession to its development and is now willing to retreat from his original premise that he has built his argument upon thus far—namely, that groups of kindred societies or communities which are of a peculiar species known as civilization would prove to be intelligible fields of study for the proper understanding of human history. By this definition he really meant that the course of the life of a civilization was self-determined in the sense that it could be studied and understood in and by itself without any necessity for allowing for the influence of alien social forces. This assumption proved to be most satisfactory for Toynbee in his study of the genesis and growth of civilizations and he felt it was equally reliable in his examination of their disintegration and breakdown, for even though a disintegration may split into fragments, each fragment is simply a part of that civilization from which it split and even the external proletariat is recruited from the elements within the sphere of influence exercised by the disintegrating civilization.

But now Toynbee is forced to admit that this assumption is no longer valid, for his survey of the fragments of a disintegrating society, the dominant minority and the internal and external proletariat, forces him to consider other factors which he calls alien inspirations. Thus he can only maintain the original definition of a society, as in his study of the process of disintegration, with reservations; for even though the breakdown of civilizations is caused by an inward loss of self-determination rather than by external factors, it is not true that the process of disintegration as a whole, through which a civilization must pass on its way to ultimate dissolution, can be understood apart from external agencies and activities.

In this process of disintegration, the substance of a society (body social) not only tends to split into three component parts, but it also resumes its freedom to enter into new combinations with elements derived from other bodies or societies. Dominant minorities and external proletariats suffer from a very definite handicap if they have an alien inspiration which causes discord and destruction, while, on the other hand, the work of an internal proletariat is quite likely to produce harmony.

As evidence of his thesis, Toynbee offers examples from the history of the Roman Empire which provided a universal state for the Hellenistic world, and also the British Raji which set up the second of two alien universal states for the Hindu civilization. Between these two universal states, however, there is a very fundamental difference. The Roman Empire as a universal state was provided by a dominant minority which was indigenous to the society for which it performed this service. As a result of this, the empire was loved and revered even when it was in a state of dissolution and was no longer able to perform those services for which it was intended. But because the British Raji was an alien universal state, it was hated by its subjects. Toynbee argues that other alien universal states have suffered the same fate as the British Raji and for the same basic reason. The Syriac state imposed by Cyrus on Babylon was so hated that in 331 B.C. the Babylonians welcomed an equally alien universal state imposed upon them by Alexander the Great. In the same manner, the

Mongol conquerors of China aroused the animosity of the Chinese in spite of the fact that they provided a sorely needed universal state for the Far East. This animosity stands in sharp contrast to the toleration with which the Chinese accepted the Manchu domination at a later date. Toynbee explains the differences in these two universal states in China by the fact that the Manchu were the "backwoodsmen" of the Far Eastern world and were, therefore, not alien.

On the other hand, in contrast to the dominant minorities and external proletariats, for the internal proletariats an alien inspiration is not a curse but a blessing which confers upon them an apparently superhuman power of taking their conquerors captive and of attaining the goal for which they were born. Toynbee tests this thesis by an examination of those higher religions and universal churches which are the characteristic work of the internal proletariat. He insists that the potency of these higher religions depends on the presence and strength of an alien spark of vitality in their spirit. The five higher religions which he considers as evidence are the worship of Osiris, the higher religion of the Egyptian proletariat with its alien origin in the Sumeric worship; the worship of Isis in which the alien spark is Egyptaic; the worship of Cybele with its Hittite background; Christianity and Mithraism, both of which Toynbee insists have an alien Syriac spark and the Mahayan with an Indian alien origin. He further claims that the first four of these higher religions were created by Egyptaic, Hittite, and Syrian populations which had been conscripted into the Hellenic proletariat as a result of the conquests of Alexander, while the fifth was created by the conquest of an Indic world by Euthydemic Bactrian Greek princes. Although these five religions differ from one another in their spiritual essence, they are all superficially alike in having an alien origin. This leads Toynbee to the conclusion that this alien spark is a help rather than a hindrance to a higher religion in winning converts and the reason for this is rather obvious. An internal proletariat, alienated from the broken-down society from which it is in the process of secession, seeks a new revelation and this is what the alien spark provides. Its newness makes it potentially attractive, but before it can become attractive, its new truth must be made intelligible. Thus Toynbee ascribes the victory which Christianity won over the Roman Empire to the efforts of the Apostle Paul and the early fathers of the church to translate Christian doctrine to the people in terms of Hellenic philosophy and to build the Christian ecclesiastical hierarchy on the pattern of the Roman civil service and to mold Christian ritual on the model of the mystery religions and even to convert pagan festivals into Christian celebrations and to replace the pagan cult of the heroes with the Christian worship of the saints. Thus, according to Toynbee, if Christianity had not been Hellenized it would not have been given a home in Greek thought and would not have achieved its status as a higher religion.

The fact that a higher religion has an alien inspiration means that the nature of that religion cannot be understood without an understanding of at least two civilizations: the civilization in whose internal proletariat the new religion arose, and the civilization from which it derived its alien inspiration. Toynbee admits that his recognition of this necessity forced him to made a radically new departure in his study of history and to surrender the basis which he had used thus far in his search for its meaning. He admits that from this new position he must transcend those limits within which he has previously carried on his study.

SCHISM IN THE SOUL

The schism in the body social is a collective experience and therefore, according to Toynbee, somewhat superficial. Its significance lies in the fact that it is an outward and visible sign of an inward and spiritual disturbance. A schism in the soul of individuals must surely underlie any schism which becomes apparent in the society of which the disturbed souls are a part. These schisms in the souls of members of a disintegrating civilization reveal themselves in a variety of forms because they arise in every one of the various types of behavior and feeling which are characteristic of those who play their part in the genesis and growth of a civilization. But in the process of disintegration each of these single lines of action is quite likely to split into a pair of mutually antithetical variations or substitutions. In this process the response to

45

a challenge is polarized into two alternatives, one active and the other passive. But neither of these is creative. A choice between the active or passive response is the only freedom left to those souls that once had the opportunity for creative action.

Toynbee is once more confronted with the problem of how to avoid what seems to be determinism in history. In order to save his doctrine of freedom for man, he insists that the soul has only lost the opportunity rather than the capacity for creative action. But this distinction is a rather fragile reed on which to find support for a doctrine of human freedom. And Tonybee is not entirely satisfied nor unmindful of its weakness as is seen in his admission that as the process of disintegration continues, the alternate choices tend to become more rigid in their limitations, more extreme in the divergence and more momentous in their consequences. Yet he offers no real solution to the difficulty and continues his arguments with an analogy between personal responses and those to be found in the collective experience of a disintegrating society. Persons may react in one of two ways, both of which are substitutes for creativity and are at the same time attempts at self-expression.

The passive reaction is abandon, in which the soul gives way to its own appetites in the belief that if it is living according to nature it will some time recover in a mysterious manner the lost art of creativity. The active alternative is a strenuous attempt at self-control by which the soul attempts to discipline its natural passions on the assumption that nature is the bane of creativity. Thus to gain a mastery over nature is the only road to the recovery of its lost creativity.

There are also two types of behavior which are substitutes for that mimesis of creative personalities which Toynbee previously described as perilous, but necessary, shortcuts on the road to social growth. The passive form of behavior is truancy and its active alternative is martyrdom. Toynbee defines the truant as one that is inspired by the genuine feeling that the cause which it serves is not really worth the price the cause demands for its services. On the other hand, he regards martyrdom as a form of escapism.

On the level of feeling, in contrast to behavior, there are also two possible reactions to a reversal of the movement of

46

élan in which he maintains the nature of growth seems to reveal itself. Both reactions are a kind of conscious retreat. The passive expression of this consciousness of continual and progressive moral retreat is the sense of drift. In this condition the soul is convinced that the universe at large is at the mercy of a power that is both irrational and irresistible. The alternative reaction is the sense of sin in the defeated and routed soul.

On the plane of life the two pairs of alternative reactions are actually variations of a single process—the transfer of the field of action from the macrocosm to the microcosm. In one pair the temper of reaction is violent and in the other gentle. Toynbee calls the passive reaction in the violent pair anarchism and the active reaction futurism. In the gentle pair the passive reaction is detachment and the active is transfiguration. He defines detachment as a spiritualization of archaism, a withdrawal into the fortress of the soul, a surrender to the world. Transfiguration is a spiritualization of futurism. It is that action of the soul which produces the higher religions.

In both archaism and futurism the attempt to live in the microcosm instead of the macrocosm is given up for the sake of pursuing a Utopia which the defeated soul finally believes he can achieve without any serious spiritual climbing. Toynbee argues that this external Utopia is a kind of other world, but only in the shallow sense that it is the negation of the macrocosm in its present state of being, here and now. The soul proposes to do its duty simply by moving from the present disintegration of society to a goal which is nothing more than the same society, as it once was or as it may yet be at some future time.

This is a profound analysis of most forms of Utopianism and there can be little doubt that Toynbee has penetrated deeply into the philosophy of liberalism and has brought to the surface its inherent shallowness of thought and its failure to adequately understand the deeper currents of history. Toynbee argues forcefully that both those who trust in either archaism or futurism must share a common fate because they are both guilty of attempting something which is contrary to the order of nature. Futurism at its worst is what

47

Toynbee calls Satanism. Archaistic or futeristic Utopias are literally "nowheres," and the "certain effect of striving out towards either of them is to produce a troubling of the waters with a violence that brings no healing" (Somervell I, p. 432).

Having now set before his readers six pairs of alternative ways of behavior, feeling, and life that present themselves to the souls of men who are members of a disintegrating society, Toynbee proceeds with his argument on the assumption that these reactions discernible in persons will also be evident in the segments of a disintegrating society. On this basis he argues that all of the four personal ways of behavior and feeling—passive abandon, the active self control, the passive sense of drift, and the active sense of sin can be seen in members of the dominant minority and the proletariat alike. On the other hand, in the case of the social ways of behavior and feeling, he distinguishes between the active and the passive pairs. The passive social phenomena—the lapse into truancy and the surrender to the sense of promiscuity—are more likely to appear first in the ranks of the proletariat and to spread from there into the membership of the dominant minority. On the other hand, the two active social phenomena, the quest of martyrdom and the awakening to a sense of unity seem to make their first appearance in the ranks of the dominant minority. Conversely, in the case of the four alternative ways of life, archaism and detachment are more characteristic of the dominant minority while futurism and transfiguration are the resort of the proletariat.

Toynbee admits that abandon and self-control are difficult to identify because of the variety of ways in which they may be expressed. The vulgar hedonists who misrepresented Epicurus previously now represent abandon in Greek life, while the Stoics are the personification of self-control. He finds in the persecution of the Christian Church by a dying Roman Empire an example of his idea of truancy and martyrdom. The truants were those traitors who surrendered their copies of the Bible to the Roman authorities to escape death, while the martyrs are those Christians who willingly faced death for their faith's sake.

The sense of sin, the passive way of feeling the loss of the *élan* of growth, Toynbee feels, is one of the most powerful of

48

the tribulations that can affect the souls of men who are called upon to live in a disintegrating society, and he even ventures the suggestion that the pain may be a punishment for the sin of worshiping the creature rather than the Creator. For those who are afflicted with this sense of drift, chance and necessity are the alternate forces of that power which seems to rule the world. Although at first glance, they may seem to be quite contradictory, Toynbee argues that they are only two faces of the same illusion. Toynbee claims that this Western belief in the omnipotence of chance produces a philosophy of laissez faire. But necessity is only another face of the Goddess Chance and the modern Western world has extended the doctrine of necessity from the field of philosophy, as it was found in Democritus and Stoicism into the field of economics, and here Marx has given to it its classic expression in his doctrine of economic determinism. But the number of those in the West who unconsciously worship this god of determinism is vastly larger than those who are conscious communists. Toynbee finds these unconscious communists in those schools of modern psychology which deny the existence of the soul and he likewise finds it expressed in the Biblical doctrine of original sin, which he calls a variant of this belief in determinism.

In spite of the position that Toynbee takes in regard to the Biblical view of sin, he finds, nevertheless, that he must somehow account for the moral vigor of Calvinists which he admits has been a puzzle to many minds. For determinism is supposed to be an enemy to that very kind of activity for which Christians have become famous. He insists that a determinist creed, whether it be that of Calvin or Marx, is an expression of drift, but he also admits that Calvinists live lives which are in contradiction to this and that they are distinguished by an "uncommon energy," purposefulness, and "assurance." The only answer he can find to this riddle is the assertion that "the addicts of predestination creeds on whom their birth has had this fortifying and stimulating effect seem all of them to have made the bold assumption that their own will was coincident with the will of God or with the law of Nature or with the decree of Necessity and was therefore bound, a priori, to prevail" (Somervell, I, p. 450). On his part, Toynbee is quite confident that both the Calvinists and the Marxists will have their bubble pricked and the only reason that it has not yet been pricked is that neither movement is old enough to have suffered this fate. He points to the weakening of the Mohammedan ability to meet present day challenges as proof of the fact that determinism ultimately destroys the morale of the people.

It is obvious at this point, as well as at many others through his *A Study of History,* that he confuses the Biblical doctrine of the sovereignty of God with philosophic determinism in such a way that he can see no difference between the determinism in the dialectical materialism of Marx and the foreordination of Calvinism, and he is thus convinced that the adherents of both systems will ultimately come to a common fate, the loss of their morale.

The active counterpart of the sense of drift is the consciousness of sin which is an alternative reaction to an identical awareness of moral defeat. In essence as well as in spirit the sense of sin and the sense of drift present a very sharp contrast to each other. While the sense of drift has the effect of an opiate, leading the soul to an insidious acceptance of evil which is assumed to reside on external conditions not subject to its control, the sense of sin, on the other hand, acts as a stimulus because it allows the sinner to think that the evil is within him and is therefore under his control if he only wills to carry out the plan of God under the operations of divine grace.

Toynbee insists that this awakening to a sense of sin can be seen in the history of Hellenism, many centuries before a Hellenic trickle mingled with a Syriac stream in the river of Christianity. As evidence he cites a well-known passage from Plato's *Republic,* saying that it almost reads as if it came from the pen of Luther. The prophets of the Old Testament furnish another example of the recognition of sin on the national level as the true cause for the misfortunes of the Children of Israel. Their teachings were taken over by the Christian Church, and in this way became a part of the Hellenic world which had been unconsciously preparing itself for the reception of the teachings of the prophets for centuries.

Promiscuity, the next form of reaction, is a passive substitute for the sense of style characteristic of civilizations in their period of growth. The sense of promiscuity manifests itself in various ways—by a vulgarism and barbarianism in manners and in art, and also by what Toynbee calls *Lingua Fran*, which is the result of the intermingling of peoples and this in turn leads to the debasement of their respective languages. But this sense of promiscuity also shows itself in a syncretism in religion in which Toynbee can discern three different phases or types—the amalgamation of different schools of philosophy, a similar development between schools of religious thought, and finally a syncretism between religion and philosophy. However, since philosophies are the contribution of the dominant minority and higher religions spring from the internal proletariat, a vulgarism takes place. Although the internal proletariat makes some few concessions to the philosophy of the dominant minority, this latter group moves much further toward the position of the internal proletariat. Toynbee's classic example of this type of syncretism is the interaction which took place between Christianity and Hellenic thought. He maintains that while Christianity employed the categories of Hellenic philosophy in which to express its theology, this was a very small concession in contrast to the great change which took place in Greek philosophy between the ages of Plato and Julian.

From this and many other such examples Toynbee is led to the conclusion that in the last act of the dissolution of a civilization, the philosophies die while the higher religions live on and stake out their claims upon the future (Somervell, I, p. 480). This is the miserable end of the philosophies of the dominant minority even while they strive to win their way into the more receptive soul of the internal proletariat. When philosophies and religion meet, the religions must increase while the philosophies must decrease.

Then Toynbee raises the question: Why must this be the case? What is the fundamental weakness that dooms a philosophy to defeat in its encounter with one of the higher religions? The answer lies in the fact that it is deficient in that spiritual vitality without which it cannot hope to attract the masses and without which it cannot command a missionary zeal on the part of its adherents.

The sense of unity is the active antithesis of the passive feeling of promiscuity as it expresses itself in the core of a universal state, which is the product of the desire for political unity, and it reaches its zenith at the time of troubles in a disintegrating society as the disintegration reaches its climax. This is the basic reason underlying the establishment of the Roman Empire and the longing for a world order of some kind in our own Western society that is evident today, even though it is meeting with little success. This active antithesis to the passive feelings of promiscuity may also inspire concepts of an omnipotent law and a sovereign God as well as the desire for a universal state. This pair of concepts, an omnipotent law and an omnipotent God, will be found at the heart of almost every representation of the universe that has ever taken the form of a universal state. But there are two distinct types of these cosmologies: in the first, law is exalted at the expense of God, while in the second God is exalted at the expense of law. The emphasis on law is characteristic of the philosophies of the dominant minorities while the religions of the internal proletariat tend to subordinate themselves and the majesty of the law to the sovereignty of God. But Toynbee feels that we must place little emphasis on these distinctions because it is only a matter of emphasis for all of these cosmologies have both of these concepts.

In the systems in which law is unduly exalted, the personality of God recedes into the background and Toynbee cites as evidence for this conclusion the fact that the triune God of the Athanasian Creed has gradually faded from an ever-increasing number of Western minds as the study of the various physical sciences has exalted the idea of natural law "until, in our own day, when science is laying claim to the whole of the spiritual as well as to the material universe, we see God the Mathematician fading right into God the Vacuum" (Somervell, I, p. 498).

Toynbee insists that the concept of a unity of all things through God as well as the alternative view of the unity of all things through law is a conception derived from the constitution which a universal state is likely to assume as it gradually crystallizes into its final shape. In this connection an interesting development takes place, however. This relationship between a universal state and a view of unity in God is accompanied by a religious revolution among the peoples absorbed by the universal state. In place of a pantheon in which a high god exercises a kind of sovereignty over many lesser deities, there appears a single God whose uniqueness is his essence. Toynbee contends that such a revolution took place in Jewish religion and that it came to its completion about 165 B.C. as a result of the Achemenian political influence over Judah.

At this point in the development of his general thesis, Toynbee displays a rather bizarre attitude towards Christianity when he turns to consider the question as to why an exclusive and provincial deity like the Yahweh of the Israelites was able to gain the supreme role in that mystery play which has as its plot the revelation of God to man. He goes so far as to call this Old Testament God barbaric and insinuates that his qualities for playing this tremendously important role were inferior to those of some of his unsuccessful competitors. This would seem to leave Toynbee in something of a quandary, but he has an answer for it. This God of the Old Testament is a living God with whom persons can have a spiritual relationship, something like that which is possible between human beings. Thus when this living God of the Scriptures encounters the abstractions of philosophy, he conquers his rivals for this very reason. The same factor held true for Christianity when it came into contact with its pagan adversaries.

Toynbee next examines archaism as a method of reaction and he defines it as the attempt to escape from an intolerable present by reconstructing an earlier period in the life of the disintegrating society. In a time of troubles these disintegrating states are idealized in a manner contrary to the facts of history and the further away they are from the present, the more they are falsely idealized. The most glaring example of this type of reaction is the cult of Teutonism in Germany which was a product of the archaistic revival of romanticism in the nineteenth century, for this cult of Teutonism ultimately gave birth to the Nazi movement of the present era.

This restort to archaism is discernible in the attempt to revive the use of languages, and likewise appears in the field of religion. Toynbee points to the Anglo-Catholic movement within the Church of England during the nineteenth century as an important example of this. Hellenic history offers an example of the use of archaism in the revival of state religion

53

in the worship of the Roman Emperor in the reign of Caesar Augustus. Toynbee concludes that an air of failure and futility surround practically all examples of archaism for the simple reason that the archaist is condemned by the very nature of his enterprise to be forever trying to reconcile the past with the present. And this is an impossible task. In making this vain effort the archaist is only playing into the hands of the futurist and his dangerous game. In this futile effort to revive the past, the archaist is actually opening the door to a ruthless innovation which has been waiting for just such an opportunity to force its way into the disintegrating society. Archaism furnishes the opportunity.

Futurism, like archaism, is an attempt to break away from an irksome present, but it differs from archaism in the direction which it takes. But in its leap forward to the future it is equally futile and a forlorn hope. In the sphere of politics, futurism may express itself in the deliberate destruction of existing landmarks or boundaries and in the forcible destruction of existing parties or sects and even the liquidation of whole classes within the society. In brief, futurism may be described as revolutionism and in art it is iconoclasm.

Toynbee admits that this resort to futurism in the political arena may at times bring a kind of success, but intrinsically it is a barren goal. However, futurism is not entirely without value to the society which embraces it for it may lead to developments which Toynbee calls detachment and transfiguration. Detachment, however, tends to be self-defeating in that its logical conclusion is suicide, and it must be eclipsed by the mystery of transfiguration. This latter development is the only one of the four ways of life which offers any real hope for society for it transfers the field of action from the macrocosm to the microcosm and this process Toynbee calls etherialization. While detachment is only a withdrawal, transfiguration is a withdrawal from society and then a' return, a palingenesia, by which Toynbee means the birth of a new species of society. He relates palingenesia to his theory of Yin-and-Yang. In the first beat of the rhythm a destructive Yang movement (disintegration) passes over into a Yin state (detachment). But it does not stop with the achievement of detachment or the peace of sheer exhaustion, for it then passes over into a creative Yang movement or Transfig-

54

uration. The double beat of Yin-and-Yang is a particular form of the general movement of withdrawal and return. For Toynbee the supreme example of withdrawal and return on the personal level is the death of Christ which is followed by his return in his kingdom, not in a futuristic sense, but in this world. There is no room for any millennialism in Toynbee's view of the kingdom of Christ.

This use of palingenesia brings Toynbee to a consideration of the relationship between deteriorating civilizations and individuals. The secession of the proletariat, the essential feature of disintegration in any society, is achieved under the leadership of creative personalities. In the process of disintegration the creative spark is not extinguished, but it is now forced into a different type of activity from that in which it was engaged during the rise of a civilization. The creative personality, must now play the role of a savior in a period of disintegration. Just why it is forced to play a different role is not explained, and it would seem that this assertion is little more than a dogmatic assumption rather than the result of empirical observation. At this point Toynbee's subjectivism comes to the forefront and he draws a conclusion which is simply not warranted by the facts.

Some of these saviors will try to save the disintegrating society itself while others will endeavor to save *from* the disintegrating society. These saviors who seek to save the society itself arise out of the dominant minority, and it is their purpose to convert the rout under way into a new advance. But the common characteristic of all such attempts is their common failure to achieve this goal. In their efforts toward war they will ultimately use force to achieve their goals and in so doing they will create a universal state.

Others, on the other hand, will attempt to save from a disintegrating society, and in spite of the difference in their methods this latter group is in agreement that it is futile to attempt to save the society. Those who seek to save from present disintegration will seek salvation in one of four possible methods. The savior archaist will try to reconstruct the past while the savior futurist will make a blind and futile jump into the future. The archaists and futurists also resort to the sword and perish by it. The savior who looks to detachment will appear on the scene as the philosopher-king.

55

And the remedy must also fail because of a basic incompatibility between the use of detachment which is an essential characteristic of the philosopher and the necessary activities of a king. On the other hand, the savior who points the way to transfiguration will appear as a god incarnate. Toynbee finds the supreme example of transfiguration in Jesus Christ who differed from all others who used this solution to the problem of disintegration because they were only men while Christ believed he was God. Only Christ conquered death. It must not be assumed that Toynbee is in any way asserting his belief in the Biblical doctrine of the Resurrection, but rather does he mean that Christ conquered death to a degree in founding a kingdom here on earth enshrining his ideals.

At the end of Volume Six in his *Study of History*, Toynbee comes to the final phase of his study of disintegration and dissolution with an investigation of the rhythm which accompanies and characterizes this process. Disintegration is not a uniform movement and there is actually less uniformity to it than there is to the process of growth. However, he fails to make it clear just why this is the case. The rhythm in disintegration may be described as a rout-rally-rout-rally-rout process. The time of troubles following a breakdown is a rout, and the establishment of the universal state is a kind of rally. The interregnum which follows the breakup of a universal state is the final rout which marks the dissolution and death of a civilization. But within the lifetime of a universal state there may be relapses which are followed by periods of partial and temporary recovery. Toynbee insisted that the anarchy which came to Rome with the death of Marcus Aurelius was followed by a rally, and he finds a similar pattern in Hellenic history between 431 and 31 B. C.

This discussion makes it necessary for Toynbee to face the problem of the present status and future of Western civilization. Has Western civilization suffered a breakdown and, if so, what stage has it now reached in its disintegration? Toynbee admits that the West has suffered a breakdown and in some places he attributes this to the Wars of Religion of the sixteenth century, while in other discussions he places it at a later date. But he also insists that the West has not yet experienced the establishment of a universal state but there is prevalent in the West a strong desire for some kind of world order which would bring the blessings of a universal state without its curse. Toynbee here reiterates his belief that a universal state is the product of salvation by the sword which is no salvation at all.

Toynbee in writing Volume Six had come to the conclusion that the West was already far advanced into its own time of troubles, and he believes these to be the perils of nationalistic warfare on the one hand, and the combined energies generated by the recently released forces of democracy and industrialism on the other. These troubles date from the French Revolution and Toynbee feels that this revolution was actually the second rout of this kind, the first being the Wars of Religion. Between these two routs there was a brief rally during the Enlightenment, but this movement was spiritually inadequate for the needs of the West and it was thus followed by another rout.

Once again Toynbee is haunted with the spectre of determinism. He answers the problem with the assurance that even if all the other civilization have followed the path that leads to destruction, "There is no known law of historic determinism that impels us to leap out of the intolerable frying pan of our time of troubles into the glow and steady fire of an universal state where we shall in due course be reduced to dust and ashes" (Somervell, I, p. 553). In the light of Toynbee's own findings this is small comfort, even if there is no known law, for there may be an unknown one. This answer gave small comfort to Toynbee himself as he was writing these concluding chapters to Volume Six on the eve of the outbreak of World War II in 1939. He admitted that the future of the West looked very dark indeed, and the swift succession of catastrophic events inspired in him grave doubts about our future.

With these observations Toynbee brought Volume Six to a close, and the next four volumes which finally appeared in 1954, are devoted to an analysis of many of the larger issues which form a basic part of the argument in the first six volumes. Such issues as universal states and churches, the contacts between civilizations in space and time and the problem of law and freedom in history are dealt with in much greater detail, and at some points, such as the role of the higher religions, a marked shift in his thinking becomes apparent.

In Volume Seven he deals with universal states and churches, and he reminds his readers that universal states arise after, rather than before, the breakdown of a civilization to whose body social they bring political unity. They are a kind of Indian summer in the history of civilizations and are the product of the dominant minority. As expressions of a rally in the general process of disintegration they bring to an end the time of troubles. Universal states are thus symptoms of social disintegration while they serve to check it. Curiously enough, the citizens of these universal states quite frequently welcome their rise and come to believe that they possess a kind of immortality, and they persist in this conviction long after the universal state has collapsed. It is for this reason that attempts are made to revive them, and this fact accounts for the emergence of the Holy Roman Empire as the ghost of the Roman Empire of antiquity. Although these universal states fail to survive in the long run and are unable to prevent the ultimate dissolution of the civilizations in which they emerge, they, nevertheless, do have a function in serving the purposes of other institutions and Toynbee believes that it is their particular function to serve the higher religions of the internal proletariat. These universal states by imposing order and uniformity over a relatively large geographical area provide what Toynbee calls a high degree of conductivity between what had previously been parochial states and also between the different classes of society. Because of the toleration which characterizes the rule of these universal states they bring with them a psychology of peace and concord which are of great help in the spread of the higher religions and in eventual establishment of a universal church and Toynbee points to the fact that the Roman Empire performed this function for the spreading of Christianity as evidence for this insight. Although the internal proletariat as the creator of the higher religions derives the principal benefit on the spiritual plane from the universal state created by the dominant minority, the external proletariat also benefits, for it is a peculiarity of the universal state that the psychology of peace which it brings in its wake frequently unfits its rulers for the task of maintaining their political heritage. As a result, aggressive neighbors, either barbarian war lords or alien civilizations, are enabled to take over the crumbling civilization. With this development the final dissolution takes place and the civilization comes to its end.

The universal state, however, bestows its greatest blessings on a universal church which generally first makes its appearance during the time of troubles. The time of troubles follows the breakdown of a civilization and comes to its full development within the frame work and with the actual aid of the institutions provided by the universal state. And again Rome offers to Toynbee the classic example of how a universal state by means of its laws, armies, widely extended citizenship and improved systems of communication offered invaluable assistance for the spread of Christianity as a universal church.

But the political leadership. of the universal state tends to dislike these universal churches, and to regard them as a kind of cancer in society since they tend to appear in decaying social bodies. Rome again offers to Toynbee the classic example of this official distrust of Christianity for this very reason. Toynbee takes Edward Gibbon to task for accepting the official Roman thesis concerning Christianity although he admits that he too had been guilty of holding a rather patronizing view of churches in their cultural activities in that they preserved a precious germ of cultural life during the perilous interregnum between the final dissolution of the one civilization and the birth of its successor. Toynbee in writing Volume Seven still feels that there is some truth to the view that the universal church serves as a chrysallis of a new civilization, but by 1952 he had also come to the conclusion that this was only a small part of the truth and that these universal churches actually played a much more important role than he had previously believed. By 1952 he had come to the conviction that the civilizations which were still alive at that time all had their background in a universal church through which each of them was affiliated to a civilization of an older generation. The Western and Orthodox Christian civilizations are affiliated through the Christian Church to the Hellenic civilization and the Far Eastern civilization can trace its ancestry back to the Sinic civilization through the Mahayana, and in the same manner the Hindu civilization owes its origin to the Indic through Hinduism. Likewise, Islam served as the chrysallis for the Iranic and Arabic civilizations from the Syriac. But Toynbee is also forced to admit that not all civilizations spring from a church in its role as a chrysallis and that other media have existed. As example of this kind of deviation he points to the Hellenic civilization which emerged from the Minoan without the aid of a universal church. This in turn leads him to a further modification of his thesis, namely that none of the civilizations of the second generation—the Hellenic, Syriac, or Indic—was affiliated to its predecessor through the medium of a church and that all the known universal churches were developed within the disintegrating bodies social of civilizations of the second generation. The evidence thus leads Toynbee to the conclusion that none of the civilizations of the third generation shows any convincing promise of producing a second crop of universal churches. He summarizes his view concerning the development of civilization with the following scheme:

1. Primitive societies.
2. Civilizations of the first generation.
3. Civilizations of the second generation.
4. Universal churches.
5. Civilizations of the third generation.

On the basis of this revision of his scheme, as it appears above, Toynbee now admits that we will have to reconsider some of his previous assumptions and admit that churches rather than civilizations have been the protagonists in history, and he suggests that this is the true Biblical approach to the interpretation of history. This in turn leads Toynbee to the further admission that civilizations of the second generation have come into being not to perform achievements of their own, and not even to reproduce their own kind in a third generation, but rather to provide for the emergence of the full-fledged higher religions and to give them a setting in which they may come to birth. Primary civilizations also had this as their main function but they failed to give birth to the higher religions. Indirectly, however, they achieved their goal in bringing forth the secondary civilizations.

60

It is quite obvious that in this amazing series of assumptions Toynbee has surrendered his empirical approach to history and has resorted to what his critics call a theodicy of history. There is no empirical evidence for his assumption that it was the function of the primary civilizations to bring forth the higher religions. Toynbee virtually admits that this is the case when he observes that they failed to perform this function. How can he empirically make the observation that it was their function when he admits that there is no evidence that they ever performed it?

Nevertheless, Toynbee at this point is now ready to offer a new interpretation of the role of churches in history, and he suggests that the rise and fall of civilizations can be compared with the revolutions of a wheel, the purpose of which is to carry forward the chariot of religion. He finds the evidence for this new approach in the history of the development of the Judaic and Mosaic roots of Christianity which he calls a part of the breakdown of the New Empire of Egypt into whose internal proletariat the Israelites had been conscripted. Although this interpretation of the history of Israel is quite contrary to the Biblical account, Toynbee is not deterred from regarding this conscription of Israel into the Egyptian external proletariat as the first step in that spiritual progress which was to culminate in the appearance of Christianity, and he says that it is the first instance known to historians of the collapse of a universal state.

"In this perspective Christianity could be seen to be the climax of a spiritual progress which had not merely survived successive secular catastrophes, but had drawn from them its cumulative inspiration" (Somervell, II, p. 89). By which Toynbee really means that the roots of Christianity are to be found in the fact that the Israelites were a part of the external proletariat of the universal state in Egypt and that Christianity drew its inspiration from these pagan sources.

This evolutionary conception of the development of Christianity leads Toynbee to a further conclusion—that the history of religion (or at least of the higher religions) appears to be unitary and progressive in contrast to the multiplicity and repetitiveness of that of civilizations. He finds his evidence for this conclusion in a dogmatic judgment that Christianity and the other three higher religions which have survived into the twentieth century have a closer affinity with each other than the contemporary civilizations can boast. He goes so far as to insist that there is a basic agreement between Christianity and the Mahayana Buddhism which he feels share the same vision of God as a self-sacrificing savior. For Toynbee the four higher religions are merely four variations on a single theme (Somervell, II, p. 89).

It is quite obvious that the theodicy which appears in the later volumes of the *Study of History* falls far short of being a Biblical world- and life-view and that Toynbee's view of Christianity is not that of the Scriptures. There is nothing unique in Christianity which is not present to the same or a similiar degree in the other higher religions. Christianity is merely one of the better and more significant visions which man has achieved of God, and it is in no sense a revealed religion. For this reason alone, if for no other, this section of Toynbee's *Study* is quite unacceptable to evangelicals, and it must be used with great care. His low view of Christianity comes to light most clearly in his prophetic suggestion that the one conceivable justification for the survival of Western civilization is that it might perform for Christianity and the other higher religions the service of providing them with a meeting ground on a world-wide scale and in bringing to them a greater awareness of their own ultimate values and beliefs in face of the revival of idolatry in modern man's peculiarly vicious corporate worship of himself in the totalitarian state.

Toynbee feels that if religion is to meet the challenge of the mid-twentieth century, it must be prepared to surrender to science all areas of intellectual activity, including those traditionally regarded as being within its own province, to which science may be able to establish a clear title. He is convinced that religion will actually gain ground for itself by surrendering to science such areas as astronomy and biology, and he also suggests that the surrender of psychology would be beneficial in that it would strip away from a Christian theology some of those anthropomorphic veils, "because in the past they have proved to be, the most tenacious of all the human barriers between the human soul and God," (Somervell,

II, p. 100). The reason for this lies in the fact that religion and science are primarily concerned with different kinds of truth.

With this observation in mind Toynbee then poses the problem as to whether the universal churches and the higher religions may not be a higher species of society, and in this connection he insists that the distinguishing mark of the church lies in the fact that it worships the one true God. This fellowship with the one true God has been attained by all the higher religions, and this achievement has given to these societies certain virtues not found in primitive societies or civilizations which have no contact with a universal church. Thus there can be no true unity in earth outside of this Commonwealth of God (*Civitas Dei*). While civilizations may be provisionally intelligible fields of study, the Commonwealth of God, is the only morally tolerable field of action. True human unity cannot be attained by the "grimly familiar knockout blow" which has been the traditional means of achieving unity in previous civilizations. Toynbee offers the suggestion that it is only in a society which worships the one true God that there is any real hope of avoiding the perils of mimesis which peril he calls the Achilles' heel in the anatomy of civilization. Mimesis, the process of social drill, is valuable as the means of insuring that the masses will follow their leaders, but in the change over from a Yin state into a Yang activity the rank and file transfer their mimesis from their creative ancestors to the creative human personalities of the living generation. But when these leaders fail, as they must, and attempt to use force to secure this popular allegiance, a great peril emerges. The only hope of avoiding this pitfall is a new transfer of mimesis from ephemeral temporal leaders to the worship of the one true God who is the source of all human creativity.

Because Toynbee at this point is able to say that the universal churches embodying the higher religions are the approximation on earth of the City of God which is of a higher spiritual order than the civilizations in which they are found, he is ready to reverse his original assumption that the role of the civilization is dominant in history and that the churches must play a subordinate role, and he now comes to a place where he admits that a new departure is necessary.

He must now deal with the civilizations in terms of churches rather than deal with churches in terms of civilizations. To try his newly achieved thesis, Toynbee turns to Christianity and maintains that the ability of the Christian church to take over from a Hellenic civilization a vocabulary of technical terms and to transform it into new uses is an example of the process of etherialization, which is the giving of spiritual meaning to terms which were formerly material in their content. But etherialization may be regarded as a sympton of growth rather than of disintegration. Thus Hellenic civilization was not an end in itself for it served as a kind of overture for the coming of Christianity.

This conclusion leads Toynbee to take one further step in recasting his theory of the relationship between civilizations and universal churches. When the life of a second generation civilization has served as an overture to the birth of a living church, the death of that civilization is not a disaster, but a proper conclusion to its life for it has fulfilled its function. Civilizations of the third generation are to be regarded as regressive from the higher religions for they tend to emancipate themselves from the higher religions which gave them birth and set out to live a new secular life of their own without reference to their own spiritual origins. Toynbee cites the eruption of our modern secular Western civilization out of the *Republica Christiana* as the classic example of such a secularization.

However, this departure of the affiliated civilization from the church is not so much the result of a desire to become secularized as it is due to a development which takes place within the higher religion in that it seeks to become institutionalized in order to become militant on earth. This, according to Toynbee, is a fatal error, and he cites the effort of Hildebrand (Gregory VII) to re-establish papal temporal supremacy as a prime example of spiritual regression resulting from institutionalism.

Another false step which the church takes also leads to a secularized civilization of the third generation. This is the idolization of itself, by which Toynbee means that it comes to regard itself as the sole depository of truth, and he again points to the history of the Roman Catholic Church during the four hundred years after the Council of Trent as concrete evidence of this very great danger.

This calamity of secularization is not the result of some *saeva necessitas* or of any other external force. Toynbee sees it as the result of "original sin" by which term he means that human personality has an innate capacity for evil as well as for good. Thus the creation of a single church militant on earth would not purge man of this original sin but rather this earth must always remain a rebellious province of the Kingdom of God (Somervell, II, p. 119).

In the final section of his *A Study of History* Toynbee pays particular attention to those encounters which takes place between civilizations, and he dwells on those encounters which Western civilization has had with Russia, Orthodox Christendom, the Hindu world, the Islamic world, and the Far East.

This shift of emphasis to a study of civilizations in encounter with each other is directly contrary to his original thesis, and Toynbee is not unaware of the contradiction. But his reason for it is to be found in his admission that while civilizations may be studied with great profit in separation from each other in their genesis, growth and breakdown, they cease to be intelligible fields of study in their final phase of disintegration. At this point they must be studied in encounter with each other. Just why this is the case is not clear, and Toynbee does not present a convincing argument.

When Toynbee comes to this study of civilizations in encounter, he focuses his attention on the West and the reader finds it difficult to avoid the feeling that the author believes that the West is nearing the final developments of disintegration although he insists that the universal state has not yet appeared. Toynbee always shies away from the logical implications of his own position. He is obviously unwilling to surrender the last glimmer of hope for the West even though his logic indicates that there is little time left for it. These last four volumes were finished in 1955, and the events of that day were forcing him to face the problem of where the West was heading in its struggle for survival. Why should the West expect to survive when its future is considered in the light of the number of failures that had been the price of each dearly bought success in the past history of the evolution of life on earth?

Yet, at the same time, Toynbee insists that on *a priori* grounds there is no reason to suppose that because all other civilizations have perished or are in a state of disintegration that the West must also perish. Toynbee is on perfectly sound ground in the light of *a priori* reasoning. But this is the point. His whole approach is empirical, and yet he looks to *a priori* reasoning when his own empirical approach leaves him little hope. His empirical observation is that war and militarism are the most important factors in the breakdown of a society and that the West has a long record of failure in its attempts to remove this cancer from its midst, even though it has achieved great success in the growth of democracy and education.

On the other hand, the evidence forces him to admit that the West faces the danger of being divided into a dominant minority and internal and external proletariats. This danger was enhanced in 1955, since Russia and the United States were the only two great powers left in the world as a result of World War II. This fact makes it absolutely necessary that war should be abolished. But the development of the atomic bomb, and its possession by the major powers makes it even more imperative that the control of atomic energy should be concentrated in the hands of a single political authority, and this monopoly of atomic power in turn compels that authority to assume the role of a world government, the effective seat of which, according to Toynbee, must be either Washington or Moscow. It is obvious that the kind of world government which Toynbee has in mind is something quite different from the form of international organization found in the United Nations. Indeed, it seems to approximate that very universal state which in his thinking represents an advanced state of disintegration in the history of a civilization. All in all, however, he offers only a faint hope for the survival of the West, and the conditions which he lays down as essential for its survival are more than offset by the development of atomic weapons and the appearance of other technological improvements which make the present dilemma far more complicated than those challenges which caused the final collapse of other civilizations. Toynbee's one hope at this point in his argument seems to lie in his belief that the Soviet Union is really the final phase of the disintegration of the Orthodox Christian society after its infection by Marxism which was imported from the West. Communism is, therefore, according to Toynbee, likely to suffer the same fate which sooner or later has overtaken all those other religions which have become militant and the prisoners of a totalitarian state because of their militancy.

TOYNBEE AND HIS CRITICS

It was almost inevitable that a work of such magnitude as *A Study of History* should call forth tremendous criticism from fellow historians. Some of it, perhaps much of it, is deserved, and yet Toynbee has been criticized almost savagely at those points at which he is least open to criticism. He has been accused of using only those facts which suit his purpose, of actually presenting a theocracy of history rather than an empirical study, and of being guilty of much factual error. One of his critics has gone on record to the effect that Toynbee's entire approach is useless and meaningless, and that he has deceived himself, if not his readers, in his affirmation of and devotion to an empirical approach to the study of history.

Savage criticisms of this kind give rise to the very definite impression that they arise not so much from a legitimate complaint against errors in factual data or the use of such facts as from an inherent hostility to the very idea of a study of history as Toynbee has undertaken it. Toynbee's basic assumption that history has meaning is an offense to some historians who seem to prefer to assume that their chosen field of professional endeavor is essentially irrational, and, therefore, without meaning. Historians who represent logical positivism and existentialism in their approach to history must be repelled by Toynbee's basic frame of reference. Between such historians and Toynbee there is no common ground on which criticism and a comparison of ideas can be carried on with mutual benefit.

There are, however, other types of criticism of Toynbee's approach to the study of history which merit attention. In the first place, there is the usual charge of factual error. And it is justified. There are factual errors in Toynbee, and this is particularly true in those fields with which he was least familiar. That such is the case should hardly be a cause for

67

surprise. But it hardly justifies the caustic comment of a critic who declared that Toynbee has ceased to be an historian except incidentally. This is far from the case. Toynbee shows an amazing knowledge of classical history and a good grasp of much of English history as well as of the events of World War I and the Treaty of Versailles. But specialists in other areas have rightly called attention to the fact that in his treatment of these other civilizations and nations he has failed to demonstrate a mastery of the facts.

A second, and more serious criticism, lies in Toynbee's interpretation of the data and his fidelity, or lack of fidelity, to his empirical approach. Many historians have rightly challenged him on this score and there can be little doubt that he has arrived at many conclusions which deny his empiricism. In fact, his whole scheme of challenge and response, breakdown, disintegration, time of troubles, and final collapse has been vigorously challenged as lacking support from the evidence which Toynbee brings forth in support of his philosophy. Many historians have frequently complained that this whole scheme is imposed on the data which Toynbee presents rather than arising from it, as he claims. And there is no doubt that he arbitrarily sets the date for the beginning of the breakdown of classical civilization in 431 B.C., and that he is equally arbitrary in his treatment of the other civilizations.

Many historians would also add that they reject his basic idea that the study of history supports his conclusion that civilizations go through the pattern which he uses in his ten volumes to describe the historical process. They not only object to what they regard as his rather dogmatic method of branding certain cultures like Judaism as fossils and others as dead. They react even more sharply to his description of the West as being in an advanced state of disintegration, even though it has not yet entered into that even more advanced sign of hopelessness which Toynbee calls the universal state. They rightly feel that Toynbee in his professed devotion to the empirical method should refrain from any type of futurism. They feel that his claim that he has escaped the snares of determinism and his struggles to avoid it are not too impressive. His futuristic conclusions are quite irritating to those historians who are so addicted to the optimism of cultural evolutionism that they cannot accept the idea that Western culture and civilization might disappear. Toynbee's forebodings concerning the future of the West are well-founded but in giving vent to them he deserted his empirical method and in so doing he unnecessarily laid himself open to the charge of inconsistency.

As devastating as the previous criticism of Toynbee's methodology may be, a still more damaging one may well be made, and this concerns the basic structure of his work and its relationship to the empirical outlook. Many of his critics have rightly pointed out that a rigid observance of this approach does not warrant the pattern of genesis, development, breakdown, disintegration and dissolution which he claims to find in the history of the civilizations which he examined, with the possible exception of our own Western. They insist that Toynbee actually has tried to take a pattern which he claims to have found empirically in his studies of Hellenistic culture and has fitted all other civilizations into this pattern, whether they actually fit or not. In support of this contention they point to the arbitrary use of dates and other factual material which occur throughout the many volumes of *A Study of History*. They further contend that the use of Hellenist culture as his frame of reference has forced Toynbee to overlook many facts which do not fit in with a preconceived interpretation of the histories of other civilizations, and an arbitrary use of the facts which he does include. This is a serious charge, and Toynbee cannot easily deny its validity. There can be little doubt that he has arbitrarily set the dates of the beginning of breakdown for his civilizations in accord with the demands of a pattern which he as superficially imposed on their respective histories in a manner which does great violence to the empirical method to which he has sworn allegiance.

This arbitrary use of a pattern derived from Hellenic civilization as the frame of reference for the study of all other civilizations has led Toynbee into other errors which have been the frequent target of professional criticism. In this connection it is pertinent to point out that some civilizations have declined because of the external violence which has been brought against them, and Toynbee is unwilling to acknowledge that civilizations have perished for such reasons, simply because this admission is contrary to his original

thesis. In a similar manner he dismisses the role of nationalism in the rise of the West. Toynbee may be correct that
civilizations rather than nations are a more fruitful area
of study, but this does not preclude the fact that nationalism
has been a very important factor in Western history since
1500, or even before, and it simply cannot be ignored because
it contradicts his basic assumptions.

Toynbee is open to still another objection in reference to
his devotion to the empirical method and this has to do with
his use of myths, not as illustrative material, for which there
might possibly be some justification, but as the basis of logical
comparison with known historical events. He actually com-
pares the creators of the Egyptian civilization in the age of
the Pyramid Builders with Zeus. This comparative use of
mythology can have no place in a study dedicated to the
empirical method. To compare the actualities of any age of
history with a Zeus who never existed in poor logic and even
poorer history.

Toynbee's frequent departures from strict historical writing into other fields of interest have produced another set
of criticisms on the part of his colleagues, some of which are
quite justified and some of which more nearly reflect the
rather narrow professionalism of the critics whose extreme
specialization frequently leads them to question the scholarship of any one who is aware of the close relationship which
must necessarily exist between cultures in their broadest aspects and professional history as such. In its most vicious form
this kind of criticism is seen in a statement to the effect that
in Toynbee's *A Study of History* there is a wealth of theory
paralleled by an almost equal poverty of subject matter. On
a more moderate level it takes the form of a charge that
Toynbee has brought together within one work a motley collection of historical insights bound together by a use of the
psychology of Jung, the philosophy of Bergson and frequent
appeals to the Scriptures. More than one critic seems to feel
that Toynbee has ceased to be a historian except incidentally.
To a certain extent there is justification for such a charge
from those historians who consciously seek to exclude all
theological and philosophical concepts from their works except
those which they smuggle in from Karl Marx. It is true that

70

Toynbee has used all these sources in an effort to interpret the data he presents, but it is hardly fair to accuse him of a poverty in subject matter. It is also true that he looks upon history primarily as political and to a degree military and omits many facts of the historical process dear to the heart of many contemporary historians, but this is not to say that he is lacking historical fact.

It is also quite natural for the logical positivists and those historians who prefer a Marxian frame of reference to be irritated with Toynbee's frequent references to religion and to accuse him of presenting a theodicy of history rather than a philosophy, but it is not becoming for them to accuse Toynbee of being only incidentally a historian simply because he does not stress the economic aspects of history to their satisfaction and ascribes to religion a role in human affairs which they cannot admit.

The violent criticism which has greeted his *A Study of History* has served to put Toynbee on trial as a historian in very much the same way that Toynbee has placed Western civilization on trial. There can be little doubt that his many critics presented to him a challenge to which he had to respond. Very few contemporary historians have been so widely and savagely criticized. Probably only the antagonistic criticism hurled against Spengler's *Decline of the West* has exceeded the intensity of that which Toynbee's monumental study has called forth. That Spengler should be criticized because of his reliance upon naturalistic determinism and ensuing pessimism along with his crushing indictment of socialism and liberalism is, perhaps, not surprising, but that Toynbee should be subjected to something of the same treatment in spite of his more optimistic evolutionary outlook is more surprising. Toynbee is consciously endeavoring to escape the foils of determinism throughout all his writings. However slim it may be, he does offer some hope of survival for the West. But this offer of hope does not appease the wrath of those who are repelled by what they feel is an inherent pessimism, even though other critics accuse him of relying too heavily upon Bergson. Quite a few of his critics are in essential agreement that in spite of his Bergsonian leanings he has not sufficiently freed himself from the shadow of Spengler, and they would even say that his alleged Augustinian outlook only strengthens the pessimism which underlies his thinking.

The foregoing indictments constitute the essence of the criticisms levelled against Toynbee by his colleagues. It would be both tedious and beyond the scope of a study such as this to examine all of them in any greater detail. Some of them are contradictory in their nature and others may be actually signs of Toynbee's own greatness as a scholar. The fact that his continued study led him to change his mind concerning the relationship which exists between universal churches and civilizations has led to the charge that he is inconsistent. But is not an inconsistency which results from a greater insight into the facts of a situation the very essence of historical scholarship, and does it not to a degree tend to contradict the other criticism that he has imposed on history a preconceived scheme to which all civilizations had to adjust?

It is quite certain that the intensity and scope of the charges laid against Toynbee have been prompted by something more than a mere professional zeal for historical exactitude and professional thoroughness. Rather is it obvious that to a great degree they have arisen from deeper forces at work in the world of scholarship and that they reflect the present state of the scholarly mind. It is difficult to escape the conclusion that the historians, political scientists, sociologists, and representatives of other specialized branches of learning have something else in view beside a criticism of Toynbee in the light of their own specialities. In many cases it has been very difficult for them to conceal their deep-seated contempt for the central theme of Toynbee's massive scholarship and that they almost resent what he has attempted to achieve.[2]

---

[2] The author finds much in Toynbee with which he cannot agree for reasons which will be set forth at length in the next section of this monograph. But at the same time, in spite of the obvious shortcomings of *A Study of History*, both in respect to actual errors of fact and the misuse of data, this author can only admire the massive assault which Toynbee has made on the accumulations of data accomplished by generations of historical research which have now reached such an amount that very few historians have both the courage and the learning necessary for finding some central theme which will give meaning to this staggering amount of what seems to be isolated facts, lacking any real reference or meaning. For many historians a narrow specialization has become a means of escape from the impossible to the possible.

It was with this in mind that Toynbee has been able and willing to do what very few historians have ever done before on such a vast scale, and this is to answer his critics. With this purpose clearly in view Toynbee wrote his *Reconsiderations* (1961) which became the twelfth volume of his great work. In this final answer Toynbee gives serious consideration and for the most part a thoughtful answer to the many criticisms made against the first ten volumes.[3] If it is true that very few historians have received so much in the way of attack for their views of history, it is equally true that no modern historian has earnestly sought to answer his critics and to accord them the treatment which they deserve as Toynbee has sought to do in this last volume.

Although this last volume is an unusual kind of book in that Toynbee does give a careful and courteous answer to his many critics, he does not make any material changes in his interpretation of history. The basic structure of the first ten volumes remains essentially intact. This is not to say that Toynbee refuses to pay any attention to the criticisms which have greeted his work for this is not the case. He admits, for instance, that the charge of using *a priori* arguments is the most serious that has been brought against him, and he admits it to be true (p. 3). He further confesses that the different elements in his Hellenic model are not all of equal value for the study of other civilizations, and he broadens his use of Hellenism to include the Sinic Civilization as another possible pattern for the study of civilizations. These two models taken together become his new basis for determining the pattern for the growth and breakdown of other civilizations (pp. 185-198).

In answer to his critics he makes his greatest concessions in his new classification of the civilizations which he finds thus far in human history (Somervell, II, 558-561). However, even these concessions do not seriously modify his basic approach. His other concessions are chiefly admissions that he has been too rigorous in some of his distinctions such as in his use of challenge and response (*Ibid.*, p. 141), and again in his comparison between primitive societies and civilizations

---

[3] Volume Eleven is actually a collection of charts and maps and is reference for the material presented in the first ten volumes.

(*Ibid.*, p. 152). Toynbee also admits in this most recent volume that he is less certain of the span of four hundred years for the duration of his universal states.

On the other hand, Toynbee is equally zealous in defending himself from many of the charges and criticisms which have been literally hurled against his works, and he points out that on more than one occasion these criticisms are mutually exclusive and contradictory. In conclusion, let it be said that he vigorously defends his basic approach to the study of history, and his scheme of genesis, growth, breakdown, disintegration and disolution remains intact.

CONCLUSION

It is ironic that many of Toynbee's critics have taken him to task for adopting an essentially Augustinian view of history. Both his critics and many evangelicals have been misled by his frequent reference to the Scriptures and his constant appeal to Biblical events in support of the various aspects of his view of history. There is no doubt that Toynbee does have a kind of religious view of history, and that he frequently refers to the Scriptures. But it does not follow that he is an Augustianian; in fact he expressly repudiates almost every doctrine upon which Augustine based his own Biblical interpretation.

Toynbee denies the uniqueness of Christianity although he admits that it is one of the higher religions. However, he insists that because it is one of the higher religions it can learn much from the other religions which he places in this same category. He admits that he was brought up to believe in the orthodox view of Christianity, and that it was a unique revelation of the whole truth. But he came to believe that all historic religions and philosophies are but partial revelations of the truth, and he now insists that Buddhism, Hinduism, Islam, and Judaism all have something to say to Christianity. It is obvious that in the light of this admission Toynbee could not write a philosophy of history which would be Augustinian or Biblical in its frame of reference.

As a matter of fact, Toynbee shifted his position while he was writing *A Study of History,* and the first six volumes present a higher view of Christianity than is found in the last

74

Sic!

four volumes which he admits he wrote more from the point of view of Buddhism and Hinduism than from any other religious insight. On more than one occasion in his study of history and in his *An Historian Looks at Religion* he shows a distinct preference for Mahayana Buddhism.

Although Toynbee frequently refers to the Old and New Testaments and seemingly pays them a high tribute, he is far from recognizing them as the inspired and infallible Word of God. They are to a degree a revelation of God as are the Sacred Writings of the other higher religions. But he does not regard them as God's exclusive and authoritative revelation of himself to man. The Scriptures represent one way in which man seeks to discover God, and they are a record of man's success in the past in his long ascent to his knowledge of a transcendental being. At times Toynbee seems to give a higher role to the Scriptures than he does to other sacred writings, but there is no consistency in his attitude toward them. They are a collection of myths and folklore along with meaningful and useful historical data, but he accepts the general outlook of higher Biblical criticism, and this reliance upon higher criticism underscores his entire treatment of Christianity in all his writings.

Inescapeably this inclusivist attitude toward Christianity and the Scriptures has a dominant influence on his religious thought. He rejects the Biblical doctrines of the sovereignty of God, divine creation, and the orthodox view of original sin. For these basic orthodox positions he substitutes an evolutionary conception of reality in general, and man in particular, which he derived in part from Robert Browning and in part from Bergson whose works came to Toynbee and the Oxford of his day "with the force of a revelation." Thus an evolutionary philosophy becomes for him his essential frame of reference even though its dominant role in Toynbee's thinking is not always evident because of his seeming reliance upon the Bible.

Thus because of his rejection of man's total depravity, Toynbee consistently fails to see the Biblical doctrine of redemption. Christ for him is a noble figure whose teachings are sublime, but he fails utterly to see the Biblical doctrine of the Atonement in terms of the crucifixion on the Cross of Calvary. The whole meaning of Christianity in its redemp-

75

tive aspects has totally escaped his attention. Toynbee professes the usual liberal admiration for Christ as the Great Teacher, or perhaps as one of the Great Teachers, but he utterly denies that he is the Son of God who gave himself on the Cross for the salvation of men.

Thus for Toynbee the Cross is a magnificent symbol of the sufferings of Christ, and Christ himself becomes an example of withdrawal and return in Toynbee's scheme of history. But there is no resurrection of the body in the Biblical meaning of the word, and Christ's return from the grave is simply the coming of his spirit to his disciples with a contagious enthusiasm which enabled them to spread the teachings of their Master.

Likewise, Toynbee frequently refers to the Church and uses it as a basic element in his whole scheme. But once again his concept of the Church falls far short of the Biblical view. It is not a divinely created, ordained, and sustained organism composed of the elect throughout all the ages, but rather is it a human institution which emerged out of the Hellenic civilization and which has given rise to Western civilization. It is obvious that Toynbee's view of the Church is a far cry from that which pervades Augustine's *The City of God*. For Toynbee the Church is an essential institution for the emergence and survival of civilizations rather than the Kingdom of God on earth in the Biblical sense.

Finally Toynbee offers no Biblical eschatology. Civilizations may come and go, rise and fall according to his theory of challenge and response, and while the fall of the civilization may have and probably will have catastrophic consequences, history has no goal. It has no ultimate end, and there is no consummation of the historical process in the second coming of Jesus Christ in triumph and in glory.

For Toynbee, as for Hegel, Marx, Spengler, and process philosophy in general, the ultimate meaning of history can only be found within the process of history itself. Although Toynbee strives valiantly to escape the snares which beset Hegel, Marx, and Spengler, his massive efforts end in ultimate failure because he refused to see that the sovereign God alone has given meaning to his creation and to all history over which he is the Lord. Once again the attempt to find the meaning of history from within has ended in failure.

76